**Uzbekistan on the
Threshold of the Twenty-First Century**

Uzbekistan on the Threshold of the Twenty-First Century

Challenges to Stability and Progress

Islam Karimov

St. Martin's Press
New York

UZBEKISTAN ON THE THRESHOLD
OF THE TWENTY-FIRST CENTURY

St. Martin's Press, Scholarly and Reference Division,
175 Fifth Avenue, New York, N.Y. 10010

First published in the United States of America in 1998
Printed in Great Britain

ISBN 0–312–21368–9

Library of Congress Cataloging in Publication Data

Karimov, I. A., 1938–
Uzbekistan on the threshold of the twenty-first century/Islam
Karimov
p.   cm.
Includes bibliographical references and index.
ISBN 0–312–21368–9 (cloth)
I. Uzbekistan – Politics and government – 1991–   2. Uzbekistan
– Economic conditions – 1991–   3. National security – Uzbekistan.
I. Title.
DK948.8657.K3747   1998
958.7086–dc21   98-14840
CIP

Contents

Preface

I am glad that through this English-language edition of my book I can present to those numerous readers who take an interest in the transformations taking place in the post-Soviet area the cardinal reforms taking place in Uzbekistan after independence, the hopes and aspirations of our people, and the aims which we want to achieve in the future.

From the mid-19th century onwards, the people of Uzbekistan were under the yoke of Tsarist Russia, and later under the yoke of the Soviet Communist Empire, which made this land of unique natural and mineral resources a mere raw-material appendix. The inexcusable depreciation of and in fact the consignment to oblivion of our ancient national traditions, language, culture and customs, as well as the artificial thrusting upon us of an alien ideology and way of life greatly damaged the development of our country.

Having now shaken off the chains of the totalitarian system, Uzbekistan has chosen the path of democratic transformation, cardinal reform in all spheres of social life, the construction of a secular and law-based state with a social orientation towards the market economy, and the renaissance of our national identity, culture and spirituality.

We inseparably link our future to integration with the world community. Uzbekistan is a part of the world system and that is why the future of our country, our people, depends entirely on the progress and development of world society and on the preservation of peace and stability on our planet.

Uzbekistan has a huge potential for the establishment and successful development of foreign economic relations for an active participation in global economic relations. One of these potentials lies in the specific geo-strategic situation of our country, which can be a bridge between the West and East. Other potentials are our valuable and needed mineral resources, our agricultural products, and our advanced economic, manufacturing and social infrastructure.

But the principal richness of Uzbekistan is its human potential – our highly educated and industrious people, who bear in themselves both ancient culture and modern knowledge.

We do not hide the fact that our young country does not only have a bright future, but unfortunately we also face real threats to our independence and national security. We know enough about them and are facing them with realism. Among them there is the threat of great-power chauvinism, which has plans of a return to the past. Another threat is religious extremism, fanaticism and Islamic fundamentalism.

The problem of ecological security remains acute because of the tragedy of the drying up of the Aral Sea, and the industrial pollution of our environment.

Many challenges to our security are general. They have an impact on the interests not only of our country, but of the whole Central Asian region. Moreover, they also have a global impact. For almost 20 years in Afghanistan, one of the immediate neighbours of Uzbekistan, the fratricidal war has been going on. This war presents a threat to the peace and stability of the whole of Central and South Asia.

Among other threats are international terrorism, the narco-business, and the illegal trade of weapons. These evils can be faced and successfully fought only by common efforts.

To my mind, the problems mentioned in this book have importance not only for Uzbekistan but for all people who think towards the future. I hope that in the readers of this book I will find supporters and like-minded people.

I hope that the publication of this book in English will contribute to further mutual understanding among peoples and will promote the development and strengthening of economic, scientific, technical and cultural relations between Uzbekistan and the nations of the world.

Islam Karimov, President of Uzbekistan,
Tashkent, 1997

Introduction

The twentieth century in the life of mankind, countries and nations is coming to an end. It is certain that many of us living in Uzbekistan, leaving aside the current problems of the realities of today, are thinking about who and what we are in this world, where we are going, where and what our place will be when mankind enters the twenty-first century.

It is important to assess and be aware of the peculiarity of the period in which we are living, and of the historical significance for the present and future of those changes that have taken place in the world recently and radically transformed the geopolitical structure and map of the world.

Newly independent states, by now a traditional collocation used by everyone, have appeared in the world; from their socialist past they have won their political independence by peaceful means and have just entered the path of independent development and renewal of social relationships. States that strive to consolidate their position among other countries of the world, to be equal among equals, to become an integral part of the vast world community. States that face complicated problems: in a short period of time to overcome the tragic consequences of a failed historical experiment and to establish a genuine democratic society in a modern market economy capable of providing adequate living standards for its people and of protecting their rights and freedoms. Uzbekistan belongs to such states.

What kind of period will the twenty-first century be for the inhabitants of Uzbekistan? To what extent will their quality of life be improved? Are we completely aware of the difficulties on the road to reform, renewal and progress that we have chosen? Do we have a sufficiently clear idea about the problems, difficulties and trials that we will face on this road?

To what extent can we accomplish the goals and tasks that primarily seek to provide a decent life for people living in this beautiful, fertile and rich land? And, of course, one of the most difficult questions is: are we aware of the threats to our stability and security?

What can we set off against these threats, and what can guarantee the stable and steady development of our society, and the maintenance of the geopolitical balance in the region where we live?

What is our country's potential for stable and steady development in the forthcoming millennium, and what can we offer for a broad and all-round mutually beneficial co-operation with all countries of the world?

It was precisely the desire to answer all these and many other questions that has inspired me to write this book. The experience of the formation and development of Uzbekistan and the other newly independent states that have emerged in the post-socialist area has unfortunately shown that there is an underestimation of the threats to security and stability. The challenges are poorly forecasted; sometimes they seem unexpected and result in huge losses, difficulties and, what is more tragic, the loss of human lives. They create an atmosphere of instability and confrontation; they impede the processes of social development and progress; they provoke among the population feelings of insecurity about the future, fear for their lives and the lives of their relatives and friends. What is more important, such unpredictable events may jeopardize the possibility of the country's realizing its political and economic choices.

With the downfall of the totalitarian system, the world stopped being bipolar. But is it safer, more stable and steadier? A critical analysis of recently formed polities at both a global and regional level reveals the following characteristics:

- an analysis of the sometimes painful process of establishing the foundations of democracy against a background of acute political struggle in a number of countries;

- the intensive rebirth of national self-identification along with the aspiration of some nations and nationalities for self-determination;
- the maintenance of conflicts on interethnic grounds;
- the devaluation of ideological dogma and the growth in various forms of political and religious extremism;
- the existence of countries with underdeveloped economies and the consequent disastrous situation for their people;
- growing economic and social differences between countries and peoples, and between social layers within the boundaries of one country.

This suggests that the world remains fragile and needs careful treatment. It has been, is and will remain in the foreseeable future extremely complicated and controversial.

Today, in order to safeguard global security and balance, the problems associated with the safe and stable development of the newly independent states have become of great significance. The rapidly changing environment and balance of power in the world, and the emergence of new sovereign states in the international arena persistently require new approaches to ensure the stability of states and nations, and the drawing up of new security patterns on the threshold of the twenty-first century.

Leaders of each sovereign state must be aware of the huge burden of duty and responsibility arising from the mandate of people whose primary desires have always been to seek the most evident reality: peace, tranquility and well-being. We have no right to forget even for a second about the responsibility we bear to future generations who will continue to build and improve the new house whose foundations we have managed to lay during these years of complicated and controversial development.

Today, the entire logic of the last years encourages us to address three basic issues that will condition Uzbekistan's future: *how should security be preserved, how should stability be secured, and how can sustainable development on the road to progress be achieved? These simple words — security, stability and sustainability — have deep meanings that we must comprehend.*

The issues of how to ensure security and of where impulses for further development are to be found constitute strategic problems which have been and will be in the focus of attention of every independent state. The Republic of Uzbekistan has already gained its own experience in the search for answers to these questions. This experience enables several general conclusions to be reached. This book attempts to provide deeper exposure of these conclusions.

What are these conclusions?

Today Uzbekistan represents not only an area with huge natural and raw material resources, but also an immense market and a place to invest capital. Our country possesses enormous intellectual, spiritual and cultural potential. This, in combination with its unique geographical location, can only create a great geopolitical and geostrategic interest, particularly at a time when a new political and economic order in the world is actively being formed.

All who take part in the process of forming a new system of international relations cannot but recognize that the balance of power on the planet will, to a great extent, depend on the choices of the newly independent states in Central Asia. Without any doubt, these choices will influence, among other things, the results of the controversial processes currently taking place within the Islamic world with all their implications for the world community as a whole.

Awareness of this fact should underpin all deliberations about the destiny and development prospects of the Republic of Uzbekistan and all of Central Asia on the threshold of the twenty-first century. Naturally, every such analytical forecast and piece of research deserves to be treated with respect. *But one thing is obvious: the region can achieve dynamic and sustainable development and be an honest partner for the world community only if stability and geopolitical balances are preserved.* The principle of preserving and maintaining internal and external balances is the only instrument acceptable today for ensuring the steady and stable development of the whole region and preventing conflicts, particularly given that the Central Asian region is a knot of various political, economic, military, transport and ecological problems. These can be solved if geopolitical balance and stability in the region are preserved. And this is, in turn, a substantial contribution towards solving the problems of global security.

4

The experience of Uzbekistan's first years of independent development proves convincingly that social, political and economic stability is a great achievement and has an unsurpassed value.

That is why the motto 'People, be watchful!' should keep sounding like an alarm bell. Take care of the things you can and should be proud of: independence, peace, interethnic and civic harmony in society. How to control our own freedom and divert the abundant hazards threatening it today in our controversial and sometimes severe world rests decisively with us.

The teaching of our great thinker of the Orient, Abu Nasr Al-Farabi (tenth century), said: Wise management of a state implies reducing and removing danger from the nation.

Now we feel satisfaction that in a short period of time we have been able to achieve much on the path to our chosen objectives. But we have to learn and have a clear vision of the problems which are likely to remain priorities for a long while. The majority of these problems originate in global trends and phenomena. It is therefore very important to make an in-depth analysis of the world around us, a world where we are not alone, where not everything depends on our will and where there are serious threats to our aspirations and objectives.

Today it seems insufficient to possess the skills to react adequately to the emerging danger to stability and security. The sustainable growth of the Republic of Uzbekistan depends decisively on how accurately and how deeply we understand the nature of the existing dangers, how promptly we detect their sources and connections, and identify appropriate methods in order to achieve stability in society.

What does national security in its broadest sense imply for Uzbekistan? What is our vision of this security?

1. Uzbekistan wholly supports one of the basic principles of the indivisibility of security, that security implies a permanent process and has no limits.

2. Ethnic, regional and local conflicts and aggressive separatism in states cause the main threat to universal security since the end of the 'cold war', especially if this kind of confrontation turns out to be a powerful instrument of political influence in the hands of some states, which seek to maintain and protect their own interests and

zones of influence or to change the strategic balance of power in their favor.

In every region the problem of maintaining security is far from theoretical. And every region has its own specific features, sources of danger and security factors.

Unaddressed and unresolved problems in any region may cause a chain reaction in the whole world, and the destabilization of the situation in any region creates a real threat of the violation of the new geopolitical balance, the contours of which are becoming clearer day by day.

3. Owing to its geopolitical situation, Uzbekistan is located in the area where the system of collective security has not yet been adjusted, and that is an additional source of emerging threat.

Uzbekistan is actually located in the strategic center of the crescent comprising the richest oil and gas reserves of the Persian Gulf, Caspian Sea and Tarim Basin, that is, in the center of energy resource fields that, in the circumstances of overall energy deficit, are expected to play a key role in the future of Euro–Asia and ultimately of the whole world.

Furthermore, we are part of the region where the interests of Russia do not coincide with those of China, India and other Eastern and Western states. Actually being located at the conjunction of these potentially very powerful Euro-Asian forces, forces which are still in the process of formation and which will undoubtedly determine the image of the twenty-first century, our territory and the territory of the whole region will also be an object of interest for such powerful countries of the Islamic world as Turkey, Pakistan, Iran and Saudi Arabia.

There is another source of threat: Uzbekistan is encircled by countries burdened with ethnic, demographic, economic and other problems, to say nothing about our common border with such hotbeds of instability in the region as Afghanistan, torn apart by internal conflicts which are encouraged by religious extremism, ethnic intolerance, drug trafficking and external forces of different kinds. The threat of an escalation of the civil war in neighboring Tajikistan has lasted since our independence. It also should be taken into consideration that these are the countries where the Uzbek diaspora is the most numerous of the diasporas.

4. Regional conflicts will last as long as such dangerous threats and challenges as terrorism, drug trafficking, an illegal arms trade and a massive violation of human rights survive. All these phenomena have no state boundaries.

5. It is our deep conviction that the practice of international relations should stipulate the right of each sovereign state (deriving from its own national interests) to identify the extent of its participation in international entities and collective agreements on security, in order to ensure its own independence and stability.

Naturally, we imply that the protection of security and the unacceptability of infringements of other states' interests should be ensured and that there should be no return to the anguish and tragedy of the military-political confrontation of the recent past.

6. Of special importance, we think, are ecological and nuclear security problems. Our desire is to declare the Central Asian region a nuclear-free zone. We are particularly worried that some neighboring states are quite open about their intention to join the ranks of nuclear weapon possessors.

The Aral Sea disaster is an issue of global proportions, affecting the interests of people in many countries and with the potential to have a deleterious effect for many generations.

Threats to security are of universal character and they imply such phenomena as political extremism, including religion, nationalism and national self-isolation, contradictions of an ethnic, interethnic, local and tribal nature, corruption and criminality, and ecological problems. In other words, the threats listed should provoke a common concern among human beings, even though they take place in various regions and vary in intensity.

This book is an attempt to analyze the nature of the challenges to the security of our country, our nation, our society and each individual citizen – challenges which endanger the course of renewal and progress, and our integration into the world community. We should bear in mind that all of history is based on challenges and responses. We have reliable guarantees to respond adequately to the challenges of history through the broadest co-operation, ranging from person-to-person relations up to the level of international integration.

We recognize and must face up to these real and potential threats. At the same time we are aware of our resources, attributes and advantages. Our raw material, and human and industrial resources serve as a solid guarantee for our internal stability and international significance.

I believe that our country has a historic chance to occupy a deserved place in world economy, politics and culture in the twenty-first century. We are opening up possibilities for world-wide co-operation for ourselves, and, what is more important, for our children and grandchildren. We are eager to help everybody who genuinely wants to learn in depth about Uzbekistan and its possibilities, and to discover for themselves the indisputable benefits that will result from co-operation with us.

As we enter the new millennium, we extend to everyone the hand of friendship and mutual understanding, symbolizing this with the words: security, stability and the sustainability of growth and development, because these realities create a solid basis for the peace, well-being and prosperity of every country, every nation, as a sine qua non for the geopolitical balance of the planet, enabling each human being to face the future bravely and with confidence.

Part I
Threats to security

Chapter One

Regional conflicts

With the end of the severe confrontation marked by the struggle between two ideological systems that affected all aspects of international life, the world around us, despite all expectations, has not become a safer place with less conflict. The formation of a new world order is accompanied by an aggravation of the smoldering old regional and subregional conflicts based on various historical, ethnic, political, religious and other motives, which within the previous framework of overall confrontation were 'extinguished' in the interests of one or other pole of power. Moreover, there is the potential threat of new regional conflicts emerging with the involvement of different external forces within the boundaries of their geostrategic ambitions.

Since our independence, the collocation 'regional conflicts' has often been heard and it has become a rather common and sinister phrase. Regional conflicts are characteristic of both the developed and developing areas of the world.

Behind the bald comments of TV reporters and impressive newspaper headlines reporting on more victims of armed clashes, millions of human destinies are lost, with pain and anguish. Will it be possible to pass by impartially the latest United Nations data which put the number of refugees all over the world today at 50 million? In 1996 13 million were registered as finding asylum in other countries. Almost 30 million people are displaced *within* their respective states, being forced to leave their homes due to civil wars. What could be more horrible than the fact that any society should become accustomed to violence and the bloody tragedy of entire nations, be they ever so far away from their national borders? Such a civil attitude of an individual conditioned by misunderstanding or complacency implies more danger than an open threat of the use of force. These attitudes are absolutely unacceptable for the citizens and the leadership of our country.

Regardless of our will or our desire, Uzbekistan, following the disintegration of the USSR, has practically turned out to be a front-line state: on the external perimeters of its borders two hotbeds of crises go on burning (the one in Afghanistan, the other in Tajiki-stan), having between them taken hundreds of thousands of human lives over the past years.

Taking into account the deep and acute crisis in Afghanistan, where the war has been going on for nearly 20 years, and the impact of this crisis on geopolitical processes at a regional and global level, the tragedy it represents is equal to that of the most large-scale and dangerous regional conflicts in the modern world. Without probing deeply into its causes and prerequisites, or the motives of the ongoing crisis in neighboring Tajikistan, it is still necessary to point out that the sustainable and safe development of Uzbekistan, providing the well-being and prosperity of its citizens, is hardly possible when tension around our Republic is periodically aggravated, when military action takes place, and when reasonable peace initiatives are hindered by the misunder-standings of the fighting factions.

The tragedy of the events in Afghanistan and Tajikistan will result in a situation where, after extended internal military and political confrontation, these countries will be brought to the brink of self-extermination and loss of statehood.

Forthcoming generations are unlikely to forgive those of our contempor-aries who caused and justified the stirring up of a stone-cold fire. History, when making its final decisions, always separates the husk from the grain and does not accept justifications like the ambitions of certain individuals who hide their own malignant wishes behind the alleged interests of the whole nation. The more the opposing sides are drawn into conflict, aggravating the antagonism, the more evident it becomes that this brings incommensurably larger losses than the supposed acquisitions which participants are hoping to gain. No objective can be justified if the fate of millions of human beings is at stake.

The destructive impact of war on society and on the state is not only apparent in economic disaster, which is a natural implication of war, but also in other spheres that are of primary importance for a nation's future. Few people would dare to say that the dissemination of hatred among co-citizens on the basis of any motives whatsoever, the flows of refugees forced to leave their households, the criminalization of society, the turning of war into the sole source of earnings, the undermining of the nation's genotype and the deprivation of the young generation of the possibility of getting primary level education can ensure the future for such a nation.

Already now, observing the events in Afghanistan and Tajikistan, it is possible to state that the conflicts taking place in these countries and the consequences of these conflicts have pushed these two states backwards for dozens of years at least, while world civilization, poised on the threshold of the year 2000, is preparing for the twenty-first century. At the same time, the champions of war try to convince their compatriots that this sacrifice is the price to be paid for a brighter future.

So, what is the threat of the regional conflicts to the well-being and the progress of the Republic? At first glance, it may seem that the confrontations taking place close to the borders of Uzbekistan have no direct connection with political, economic and social stability within our state. Of no less political and civic myopia is the opinion that in the future the alarming developments will roll on smoothly avoiding our country, that stability will be preserved of itself and that the future of the country will be secured automatically.

Here I can only remark that such 'optimists' cannot imagine the huge efforts it really costs the state to secure peace and order, and to prevent the spilling over of the conflicts and adverse developments on to our soil. It is appropriate to recall here the well-known truth that if acute problems, including those that surround us, are ignored, they lead to a crisis, and an unmanageable crisis in its development sooner or later grows into a destructive cataclysm rejecting state borders and other political, economic, and ethnic realities.

In the existing environment of regional crises, the threat to the security of Uzbekistan is not hypothetical, its existence is obvious. It comes into sharp focus if regional confrontation is not just understood as armed antagonism between fighting sides within a limited area giving rise to numerous victims among the civilian population, but is analyzed from the point of view of how this situation of opposition influences all aspects of life in a particular society and its neighboring states.

The historical development of human civilization, especially in the context of the modern world, is towards full interdependency. This means that any confrontation in a separate state cannot stay within its national borders for long. For various reasons, such a confrontation will inevitably tend to spread in an incontrolled manner that sooner or later presents neighboring states with a complex of problems that lead to the destabilization of the situation in the region. From this point of view a crisis is aggravated as a rule by the overt or covert internationalization of the conflict, because there are always external forces pursuing different aims and trying to secure their own interests in the area of crisis.

So it is erroneous to analyze an internal conflict in any isolated state, and the interrelation between that state and its neighbors, as unrelated phenomena. The military and political crisis in Afghanistan and the instability in Tajikistan can only have a negative impact on both the regional stability of Central Asia as a whole and the national security of Uzbekistan in particular.

I think there is no need to theorize at length or to make references to the historical background of other regional conflicts to confirm this truth concerning our situation. It is my deep belief that the aggravation of the situation in Afghanistan in September and October 1996 demonstrates the realities and acuteness of this many-sided problem, the echo of which was felt by everyone in the country, and made us pensive about the price of peace in the Republic and the well-being of the nation. In this context it would be logical to go on with the thought that, unless the regional conflicts are settled, no state in Central Asia will be safe and able to advance confidently into the future.

The list of threats, both actual and potential, would appear to be rather long.

Firstly, special attention should be paid to the development of such situations as the deliberate or involuntary expansion of armed or other undermining activity on the territory of neighboring states, since the Afghan and, to some extent, Tajik conflicts have already reached the stage where they are actually unmanageable. In such situations the particularities of the location of the principal cultures in the area, the proportions of which vary in all Central Asian states and reveal a historically shaped interrelationship in various spheres and on various levels (including multiple relative links), should be taken into consideration.

Due to the level of ethnic heterogeneity of each of the Central Asian states any aggravation of the crises can only undermine civic harmony and stability in neighboring countries. The attempts of certain subversive groups to fan the flames of conflict and carry the crises across to neighboring countries by appealing to the national feelings of ethnic population groups living in those countries can only cause alarm.

Modern history clearly shows that forces trying to play the 'national card' for their own political and other purposes primarily draw on the high sensitivity of people's emotions in order to direct them further along the path of militant aggression, which excludes political wisdom and common sense.

Secondly, during recent years events have taken a dramatic course because in the Afghan crisis, alongside the existing ethnic factions, a religious aspect has been introduced. A strong politicization of Islam has taken place that has shaped extremely radical forms: open pretensions to power and the wish to achieve it through using arms and calling up all co-religionists in support. This process, which has nothing to do with the humane ideals and foundations of our religion, negatively influences the social and political situation over a vast area from Gorny Badakhshan to the Caspian Sea. Unfortunately, it should be remembered that, in some countries of the region, extremist elements who will not hesitate to impose the Afghan scenario on their people in total disregard of the consequences of the events in Afghanistan still exist. We and our descendants will have to evaluate this tragedy in the future.

Thirdly, centrifugal waves from the Afghan conflict, the roots of which also lie in the ethnic and confessional ambitions of various Afghan groups to seize power, continue to have a negative effect on the entire region and to take tangible shape. This is clearly illustrated by the armed provocation on the Tajik–Afghan border which, together with other manifestations of subversive activity from the territory of the Islamic State of Afghanistan, is seriously destabilizing the situation in Tajikistan and consequently in this region. In such conditions heterogeneous 'fighters for faith', to justify their actions and intentions, use religious slogans, trying to impose spiritual ideals and values alien to our nations, to sow seeds of discord and medieval obscurancy, and to deprive us of an adequate place in the architecture of human civilization.

Finally, one more potential threat deserves particular attention. The ongoing conflicts give some people the opportunity to exaggerate the problems of 'separated nations'. Often a deliberate selection of arguments is presented in favor of, for instance, the unification of Tajiks or Uzbeks and Pushtun tribes on both sides of the border with Afghanistan. The consequences of any attempt to change existing borders using the principles of ethnic division are unthinkable. A change of borders in our region might result in a horrifying effect for the entire world community, and the conflict of a similar kind in Bosnia and Herzegovina would seem a prelude to this holocaust.

Extended regional conflicts generate a wide range of problems for neighboring countries (naturally, Uzbekistan is no exception) and not only of an immediate nature. In the future, they may produce the effect of a 'delayed-action mine' in politics, ideology and interethnic relationships.

The consequences of regional conflicts have a more definite, tangible form and influence both national economies and the economic links between the states. These are not abstract concepts, they affect the interests of every citizen and community member and are easily calculated. For example:

1. The war in Afghanistan, having almost destroyed the country's insufficiently developed economy, is today the major constraint for new transport links which would allow the Central Asian states to have access to 'warm sea' ports and would help to integrate them

into the existing system of world trade. This, consequently, holds back the development of national economies, because it is a well-known fact that the shortest and most stable transport links are necessary for an effective commodities exchange.

2. There is the problem of refugees, who in the case of armed confrontations are ready 'to flood' the territory of neighboring countries. Frequently, in inflows of this sort, it is not just those seeking food and shelter who cross the border; there are also those who confuse people's souls. For the host country, this problem has an economic aspect along with the natural humanitarian one because the need arises to find additional funds from the budget to locate refugees, to provide accommodation and to solve a great deal of their urgent problems.

3. As far as the negative factors associated with the extended conflicts in Afghanistan and Tajikistan and of their great danger to neighboring states are concerned, I cannot but highlight such problems as illegal drug trafficking, international terrorism and arms smuggling. It is well known that in situations of economic devastation and political chaos military actions are not only the sole forms of business for ordinary people, but actually become one of the means of survival. Rival groups, particularly in Afghanistan, regard drug production and sale as the most appropriate means to earn money to purchase armaments and to enrich themselves. According to some international and UN evaluations, Afghanistan has not only become one of the leading producers of raw opium, but it is also the biggest transit point for ever-growing drug deliveries to the states of Central Asia and the West. Naturally, some of the drugs 'are accumulated' in our region, causing an increase in criminal activity that seduces our youth and undermines the genotype of the nation.

4. A delayed solution to the regional crises in Afghanistan and Tajikistan has also presented the states of the region, including Uzbekistan, with new and no less dangerous problems related to the expansion into neighboring territories of such phenomena as terrorism and arms smuggling. National security and internal stability depend, to a great extent, on a solution to these

problems. Similarities with the Middle East and other crises in different areas of the planet, as well as known events in the territory of the CIS countries (Chechnya, Nagorny Karabakh, Abkhazia and others), make it possible to see how terrorist activities might spill over beyond the national borders of Afghanistan and Tajikistan. The border transparency between the Central Asian states – with Afghanistan, its territory and borders turned into uncontrollable armament stocks – would facilitate this spill-over. It is difficult to deny the possibility that armed militants, after being trained or having gained experience in guerrilla war in the territory of Afghanistan, have taken an active part in armed conflicts in many countries of the world, including the Caucasus, Chechnya and Tajikistan.

The regional conflicts in Afghanistan and Tajikistan, posing real external threats to our national security, do not help to strengthen stability in Central Asia or globally. They imply considerable negative potential and could lead to disastrous effects on a global scale.

Every sober-minded man, not only in the Central Asian region but also outside it, is aware that a further escalation of regional conflicts can only influence and affect the decisions of countries in this region. How will these countries be affected? Which way will their social and political development go? What are the prospects for democratic and market reforms on which the destiny of millions of people on the eve and in the dawn of the twenty-first century depend?

The main result of the end of the 'cold war' period was that mankind had managed to escape a third world war. Do we have enough wisdom, experience and persistency to localize and neutralize the global consequences of the regional conflicts as well as the conflict in Afghanistan and the confrontation in Tajikistan?

Uzbekistan, purposefully employing all existing options both within its state policy and within the mechanisms of international institutions, has rendered and will render its support and assistance to any efforts and practical steps aimed at a peaceful settlement of and the prevention of military-political conflicts in our neighboring countries. That is the sense and essence of one of the main lines of our general national strategy.

Chapter Two

Religious extremism and fundamentalism

The end of the twentieth century – the century of astonishing scientific inventions, of man's penetration into the mysteries of the universe, of information and amazing technical opportunities – has become, even though it sounds paradoxical, a period of renaissance for religious values, a period of return to quiet, peaceful spirituality.

Islam, one of the major world religions, is no exception to this global trend. On the contrary, events that have taken place in recent decades both in the Muslim and non-Muslim worlds have given us grounds to start talking about a so-called 'Islamic boom' in the world community.

Numerous politicians, scholars and journalists have tried to offer their understanding of the reasons for this phenomenon at the end of the twentieth century, a phenomenon which has been given various names: 'Islamic renaissance', 'reislamization', 'phenomenon of Islam', etc. Without debating these concepts, it is necessary to focus attention on the events associated with the rebirth of Islamic values, which are very diversified, many-sided, sometimes controversial and even contradictory.

It is obvious that the great interest of world public opinion in these processes is accompanied by an evident feeling of alertness, and even caution, with regard to such excessive manifestations as religious extremism and fundamentalism. Unfortunately, modern history has accumulated many facts to testify that these extremely radical manifestations give rise to serious conflicts and contradictions, and threaten stability and security. That is why mankind is scared. Such manifestations provoke in us grave anxiety from the point of view of the need to strengthen Uzbekistan's sovereignty and to ensure its security.

Before we proceed to a direct analysis of the potential threats endangering our region implicit in religious extremism and fundamentalism, I would like to draw attention to some highly delicate aspects of the problems connected with the religious beliefs of people, in order to make clear the difference between the spiritual values of religion and certain ambitions – political and other aggressive goals – which are far from religious, which certain forces try to make us achieve using slogans, *inter alia* the Islamic revival.

The very fact of the stable existence of religions, including Islam, for millennia testifies that they have deep roots in human nature and perform a set of essential functions. Being predominantly the spiritual sphere of society, groups and individuals, religion has absorbed and reflects universal norms of morality, making them compulsory standards of behavior. It has considerably influenced culture and has helped/is helping to overcome human isolation and alienation from other human beings.

What is more, religion (we have grounds to state this using the example of Islam, the religion of our ancestors) strengthens people's faith, purifies and elevates, and makes them stronger in overcoming the trials of human existence; it has also contributed to, and sometimes been the sole means of preserving and transferring, universal and spiritual values from generation to generation. That is why religion is a reliable companion to human beings, and a natural part of human life.

While acknowledging the important role of religion, it should be pointed out at the same time that the religious conception of the world has not been the only way of thinking about man's attitude towards the world and towards his kind. Parallel with this, and with the same right to existence, has been the development of what is usually called secular thinking or a secular way of living.

Perhaps it is precisely this coexistence of different attitudes, unfortunately not always peaceful in comprehending the reason for living, that has promoted the richness and variety of the human world. Its spiritual activity is a stimulus to its development, because a society composed of similarly reasoning people would become gray instead of multicolored.

In the present-day world, which affirms the worth and priority of each human being, of each personality, this contradiction has been transformed into the recognition of his right to freedom of thought, to freedom to profess any religion or not to profess any. Human beings are unable, for natural reasons, to choose their race or ethnic identity, or to select their parents, but their world outlook and their spiritual and moral choices can and must be made privately without anybody's pressure or enforcement. And this choice should be respected.

Religion, as a component of social life, is linked inextricably with other spheres of social life, exerting influence but also influenced by the impact of social pressures. It is not accidental that most of the religious systems existing today were formed during periods of social, economic and political revolution and crisis. This shows that religion has, throughout human history, been employed to a greater or lesser degree to achieve political goals which were not always noble.

Unfortunately, the history of mankind has many examples of people's faith, a component of religious consciousness, being used not as a constructive power, but as a destructive force, as fanatism, which is characterized by such features or manifestations as a passionate conviction in the veracity of only one confession and an accompanying intolerance towards all others.

Precisely those people or groups of people who are guilty of fanatism are capable of generating the greatest destabilization in society because, by painting such movements as 'people's actions', they enable the population to relinquish feelings of personal responsibility for individual actions.

An unconditional confidence in the ownership of a monopoly in truth can become the ground for the growth of religious extremism, which is characterized by an inclination to radical violent actions. The targets for such actions may be chosen either from among individuals and social groups of heterodoxies or from among members of the same confession who are rejected by representatives of similar faith.

It would be fair to recognize that 'upheavals' of religious fanatism do not originate only in religious contradictions in themselves, but predominantly in unsolved social, political and economic problems. Strictly speaking, the same problems cause fanaticisms of other kinds, for example the fanaticism of Bolsheviks and nationalists.

Any religious system of itself is not able to make any recommendations on the settlement of social and economic problems. No religious system contains concrete measures corresponding to the modern level of world development, and the religious fundamentalists' appeal to a return to the circumstances in which the religions originated may hardly be considered as constructive and viable.

The phenomenon of religious revival during recent decades has become evident in the so-called post-Soviet area. Of course, religious life has never stood still; even under the administrative-command system it acquired quite specific forms. But the end of the eighties and the beginning of the nineties became a period of religious revival in society on the one hand, and of the formation of prerequisites for religion-based conflicts on the other.

The importance of this problem demands a thorough analysis of the causes behind the rise of the Islamic factor in all its diversity in our region during the period of the establishing and strengthening of state sovereignty of countries within the region.

Firstly, there was the crushing of the former system of ideological concepts and values and the need to fill a temporary vacuum.

It is common knowledge that the communist ideology – which lacks spirituality, is fanatical and anti-national in character – contributed greatly to the formation of the prerequisites for religious fundamentalism and traditionalism within post-Soviet space. This spread not only to Islam, but also to Judaism and Christianity (Russian Orthodox, Roman Catholic, Armenian-Gregorian, Protestant-Lutheran, Baptist).

All these we could witness in Uzbekistan as a sample, where over 100 nationalities and nations, and almost 15 religious confessions are represented.

The ruling communist party of the former USSR regarded the religious confessional communities as their rivals in the struggle for people's minds and throughout its entire history resorted to severe measures aimed at curbing religion, and subordinating its few surviving clergy.

Thousands of Islamic religious devotees were subjected to repression. Thousands of mosques and hundreds of *madrasahs*, which were buildings of great architectural and historical significance for our people and world civilization, were destroyed. The bulk of believers had no access to the Koran until the mid nineties. Religion was deliberately exploited as a weapon in the ideological struggle.

For the same reasons in the former Soviet Republics of Central Asia, where Islamic education was banned, only a small number of highly educated Islamic teachers could exist. Instead there flourished all kinds of superstitions, sometimes reactionary, which still today from time to time claim to possess the higher truth, and try to impose it on the entire population and to control the people's destiny.

At present and in the future we, the people of Uzbekistan, do not want to tolerate either the sad experience of the Soviet era or the new extreme manifestations that we have witnessed during the first years of our independence.

Secondly, there is the growth of national self-consciousness and the attempt to nurture an ethnic self-identification — major elements which have traditionally been regarded as the components of a well-defined religious orientation.

There is an interesting concept elaborated by Western European experts about the role of religion, specifically of Islam, in the newly independent states of Central Asia. According to their evaluations (views from outside are often better and more useful than the reflection in one's own mirror), during the period of national identification of the peoples of Central Asia Islam is able to perform two very controversial functions:

- *On the one hand*, the cultural values of Islam, its traditions and its huge spiritual heritage greatly contribute not only to the historical evolution of our region, but also to the qualitative shaping of its new image.

23

- *On the other hand,* as an instrument in the political struggle for control and influence over the political mind of the masses, Islam is able to play the role of a banner under which forces are united that do not pursue definite program objectives, but are guided by only one goal – that is the struggle for power.

Thirdly, and probably most importantly, there are dramatic changes in the social, political and economic spheres.

The unavoidable losses caused by reforms during the transition period, the objective processes of differentiation within the population and natural distinctions of ownership level have forced part of the population to take the attitude of a Soviet-like mentality in calling for a return to utopia and illusory equality, and to the pseudo-struggle against luxury and excessiveness – a return in essence to the equally-leveled standards that make people flat and society uncolored – instead of applying and developing their own skills and knowledge in order to improve their well-being. In these circumstances ideas such as Wahhabism become deceptively attractive.

In periods of stagnation, crises and splits in society the popularity of ideas inherent in Wahhabism reveals itself in the advocacy of justice, in the demands for the strict observance of Islamic ethics, and in the rejection of luxury and greed. It is unfortunate that such slogans have received support and continue to spread in a number of areas of Central Asia in recent years.

Fourthly, Uzbekistan and other Central Asian states constitute an integral part of the very complicated and multi-dimensional Islamic world. It is a well-known fact that in the world many formal and informal movements exist which use Islam for their political purposes. Some of them promote the exclusiveness of Islam, show intolerance towards all other religions, and use Islam as a platform to defend narrow-minded national interests. Their intention to involve the newly independent states of Central Asia as their political supporters and allies and exercise influence upon them is typical of their ideological purposes, which are manifested in well-defined action.

The above reasons for the growth in strength of the Islamic factor are absolutely essential for an understanding of the growth of religious activity in Uzbekistan.

Today in the Republic there are 15 confessional communities, some of which are non-traditional for Uzbekistan. The secular state attitude towards them is guided by the following principles:

- respect for the religious feelings of believers;
- recognition that religious convictions are the private practice of citizens or their communities;
- guarantee of equal rights and prohibition of persecution both of citizens professing religions and those who do not profess;
- need for dialogue with different religious associations to utilize their possibilities for the promotion of spiritual revival and universal moral values;
- recognition of the inadmissibility of using religion for destructive purposes.

This final principle corresponds to Article 18 of the International Convention on Civil and Political Rights, which upholds the right of every human being to freedom of thought and of faith, and adds that: 'Freedom to profess a faith or believe may be limited pursuant to the provisions of the Law to provide social security and safety, public order, health, and to protect the moral and major rights and freedoms of other people.'

The above quotation quite clearly separates religion as a part of spirituality and culture from an attempt 'to play the religious card' for certain political aims.

We support the idea that religion should accomplish its role in introducing the highest spiritual, moral and ethical values, and in forming a part of the historical and cultural heritage among the population. And we will never allow religious slogans to be put on the banner in the struggle for power – a pretext for intervention in politics, economy and legislation – because in this we see a serious potential threat to the stability and security of our state.

How is the threat of Islamic fundamentalism manifested in Uzbekistan?

1. In attempts to disseminate fundamentalism to undermine the confidence of faithful Muslims in the reforming state, and to destroy the stability and national, civic and interethnic harmony

that are fundamental pre-conditions of transformations for the better. Islamists are aiming to discredit democracy, the secular state, and a multi-national and multi-confessional society.

2. In the clear-cut notion that those, particularly our youth, who follow the populist, attractive, but entirely hollow and baseless slogans of the fundamentalists about justice will turn out to be hostages of the will of others, which in the end will direct not only their brains, but also their destiny. The subordination to such authority may result in personal tragedy. The most severe consequences are personal servility, constraint, slavery of an individual, complete limitation of freedom — with which our movement forward progress is impossible.

3. In provoking, among social groups and regions of the population, confrontation based on 'true' and 'false' devotional principles of religiousness. These sorts of activities led to the split of the nation in Algeria and Afghanistan.

4. In the situation of the civil war on the southern borders of Uzbekistan and in neighboring countries which is reproducing new generations of terrorists, armed militants who consider themselves to be true Muslims, fighters for faith, and those who are eager to impose their monstrous ideas on our people.

5. In creating a repulsive image of Uzbekistan among both Muslim and non-Muslim states, to whom we are presented either as anti-religious atheists or as hidden supporters of state Islamization.

6. In shaping a global confrontation between Islamic and non-Islamic civilizations. This has a most negative impact on our integrational processes within the world community and preserves the backwardness of the newly independent states. And, what is worse, people's expectation of 'civilization clashes' is based on religious principles.

7. In exerting influence on the mass mind, the concept of religion being presented as a universal means to solve all economic, political and international problems and contradictions.

Recently, there were foreign press reports that the Uzbekistan leadership does not believe in the threat of fundamentalism but uses it to frighten the West and pursue particular goals.

Among some Western analysts and Islamic scholars it has become increasingly popular to treat fundamentalism as something not harmful to the world community, as something primarily directed against the fundamentalists' 'own' states. Supposedly, the Islamists would be better prepared for a dialogue with the world community if they destroyed and rebuilt their states according to their own models. Such experts go into raptures that a high proportion of fundamentalists have received higher technical or medical education in European and American universities. Do these people fully comprehend the real situation in the Muslim East, repeatedly subject to disintegration, discord and humiliation?

Not sharing such views, I judge it necessary to focus on another side of the problem.

When reflecting on the threat of Islamic fundamentalism, we are constantly compelled to look not only at its internal Islamic causes, but also at the factors which provoke and stimulate it. These factors are well known: colonialism and neo-colonialism, great-power chauvinism and anti-Muslim diktat in international relationships, the 'divide and rule' policy. Economic discrimination, arrogance and an unwillingness fully to understand the advantages of another culture, another civilization (which in our country has the centuries-old roots of an Islamic civilization), constitute a part of the thinking of the West about the East.

However, attempts to use the idea of the exclusiveness of the Islamic world to steer it towards solidarity with other powers of the modern world in order to establish a balance of power with the USA and Western Europe are also hopeless. Such variants have already been tried in the 1950s–80s. Is there any need to carry them over to the twenty-first century?

At the same time representatives of the developed countries should understand the painful character of the present breakdown of the traditional social relations, way of life and world outlook that are so valuable for Muslims. It would be fatal for the history of the twenty-first century if Islam and the states of Islamic culture were to be represented as a new 'empire of evil' and an overall zone of danger.

It is however gratifying to learn that progressively minded personalities of the West highly appreciate Islam's contribution to

27

the flourishing of both their own and world civilization, and consider that it is high time to pay back the debts, and help development in a spiritual community where almost one billion people live.

Influential, authoritative and prestigious world forces, who stand against religious fundamentalism of any form, understand the role and importance of Uzbekistan in this struggle for normal, peaceful and mutually beneficial conditions, for the coexistence of different cultures and civilizations. They understand and support our country on its own path to reforms.

This should be remembered and appreciated by our citizens, and especially by our youth: remembering and understanding their responsibility to our state and to the world community.

Chapter Three

Great-power chauvinism and aggressive nationalism

At the turn of the twenty-first century the newly independent states face enormous internal and external difficulties. Relying on their internal resources and possibilities, they are searching for solutions to these problems with the support of interested parties in the world community. Their desire and willingness to co-operate with those neighboring countries connected with centuries-old relations that are tied up with humanitarian, informational and economic aspects is quite natural. We are not in a position to simplify here any of these rather complicated problems that have emerged since the collapse of the USSR.

Leaving aside a discussion of the objective difficulties and controversial aspects of setting up and establishing equal and mutually beneficial co-operation among the newly independent states, it is important, in my view, to pay attention to a number of artificially created problems. I would list these problems as being of subjective character originating in the unwillingness or simple inability of certain political forces to understand the objective course of historical processes, in feelings that are deeply rooted in their minds that it is their special historical mission to have superiority over other nations. It is far from our intention to generalize and draw any historical parallels and to complicate matters by referring to some nations and nationalities. But in the modern environment of setting up new civilized interstate relationships this must be considered as a factor constraining this process. Among the problems that call for the attention not only of the new states but also of the international co-operative community are, above all, those that originate in recurrences of the imperial way of thinking and behavior.

The Republic of Uzbekistan is no exception to this trend, and the past years of independent development give grounds to consider the potential threat to the stability and sovereignty of our state which is revealed through slogans, comments and actions under the definition of great-power chauvinism and aggressive nationalism.

This phenomenon is far from new in the history of mankind, which has numerous illustrations of major states and nations wishing to establish relations with neighboring countries from a position of superiority and exclusiveness. Such an approach has more than once led to large-scale clashes, bloody conflicts and wars, and raised suspicions in interrelationships which unfortunately have been transmitted from generation to generation between nations.

It might seem that, on the threshold of the twenty-first century, mankind would have accumulated enough wisdom to reject centuries-old stereotypes in the light of historical experience and recognize not only the obvious diversity and multi-dimensionality of the modern world community, but also equality between all peoples and entities as a natural and essential condition for the development of world civilization.

Nevertheless, the chauvinistic and aggressive nationalistic inertia is still dominant, which just pretends not to see what a threat it poses not only to what it is targeted at, but also to itself.

The same historical experience teaches that none of the allegedly high motives are able to justify the actions of those politicians and people who are breaking through into big politics, who are trying to boost the well-being of their nation through the limitation and restriction of other nations' rights. As long as such activities recur, we need to be on our guard.

How do we deal with great-power chauvinism and aggressive nationalism? What are their manifestations nowadays?

By looking at historical practices, this phenomenon may be

characterized as a political, ideological and economic hegemony established between concrete state forces, or an aspiration to such a hegemony based on interethnic, interstate and regional relationships. Chauvinism is revealed in the struggle of some large nations to establish their exclusive domination not only within the patterns of a multinational empire, but also within surrounding geopolitical areas. States with smaller territories, and mostly with weak economic potential and internal instability, as a rule become the objects of such claims.

The deep roots of great-power chauvinism grow due to an unpreparedness to establish civilized interactions with other nations and states. Its champions were military empires which cynically exploited the vital resources of their conquered territories. At the same time, the destructive ideas of cultural and national inferiority were instilled in subjugated nations.

Our area did not avoid such a destiny, and for a long time it experienced the fatal consequences of chauvinistic and aggressive nationalistic ideas. Uzbekistan has survived a complicated period of forced retention within the Russian and the Soviet Empires. Today this period is interpreted from different points of view, and sometimes it is given mutually exclusive interpretations.

There are grounds to say that numerous comments made on the events taking place in Central Asia are influenced by certain political and ideological intentions. Among the disseminated opinions on this topic two categories may be identified which do not reflect the whole spectrum of 'recipe' for Central Asia, but characterize very well their authors. The representatives of the first group say, and perhaps they are sincere, that the development of the region, represented as Turkestan autonomy within the Russian Empire, received the necessary impulses from its metropolis because Tsarist Russia stimulated the bourgeois evolution of the region without breaking local traditions and foundations.

The Bolshevik experiment in the region, consisting of state-ethnic delimitation, suppression and restriction of the traditional forms of social design, and a hypertrophied specialization of the economy, is severely criticized by this group of authors. They treat it as one of the principal reasons for the contradictions that exist today in

Central Asia. According to this logic, the renewed post-communist Russia is best placed to bring stability to the region.

According to the second evaluation, the region's complicated problems originate in the long colonial past of the area which introduced alien elements absolutely incompatible with the mentality of the Muslim population. The escape from this situation is a return to historical and national roots, which are realistic only if the states of the region are primarily oriented towards their neighboring Muslim countries with a view to further close integration.

However, both these scenarios involve more politics and emotions than an integrated and scientific theory. Despite the presence of features of formal logic in the debates mentioned, their authors represent extreme views deriving from numerous examples of great-power chauvinism and aggressive nationalism.

Of course, it is impossible to deny that big empires which conquered and subordinated other countries and nations implemented, to a certain extent, an educational mission in those areas which were lagging behind the world in their standard of development. Defenders of such an evaluation emphasize the contributions made by the empires to the development of infrastructure, the development of separate industrial branches, the training of national professional experts, and the introduction of the population of the conquered countries into new areas of activity and world culture.

It is difficult to deny this, but the processes of interaction between great empires and small nations have their reverse sides and the negative implications of these were much greater than the results of the inside cultivation of a civilization from the outside.

Firstly, all efforts directed to the development of colonies and semi-colonies were subordinated to the prevailing and long-term interests of the great powers. From this point of view, the interests of subordinated nations were always of secondary importance. The development of the dependent countries was always strictly controlled and was carried out in a predetermined way within the framework of the Empire's own interests. Specifically, changes in the infrastructure of Central Asia, such as the construction of roads, the development of a communications system, and the training of national professionals oriented to the Empire, were implemented only to the extent that was necessary to ensure the interests of the Empire, in this case to facilitate access to cheap sources of raw materials and energy.

Secondly, the so-called civilizational mission not only gave birth to and strengthened the destructive mentality of imperial exclusiveness and neglected the colonies, but in turn resulted in a reaction, especially in cases when such civilization was introduced by force, and thus was accompanied by a slighting of national pride, by a disparagement of national cultural and spiritual values, and even by the physical liquidation of their holders.

Finally, the deeply rooted habit to administer and instruct, the belief in one's own infallibility, may drive one to adopt strategically erroneous decisions, whose consequences serve as explosive materials for the Empire itself. A good illustration of this is the destiny of both the Tsarist and the Soviet powers.

In debating the negative potential that is rooted in the psychology and policy of chauvinistically minded persons, it is necessary to pay attention to a number of other threats which are presented at global level.

Chauvinism, and history has proved this repeatedly, stimulates the setting up and strengthening of authoritarian regimes, and leads to harsh dictatorships, because otherwise it is impossible to exercise control not only over the subordinated and dependent nations, but also the home population as well, some part of whom are inevitably against such policy.

The historical perniciousness of chauvinism is conditioned by the fact that the hypertrophied great-power syndrome, which is based on a conviction of national superiority, is built on violence, which in turn leads to numerous victims and losses in the great-power chauvinistic and aggressive nationalistic states.

In this connection, it is right to affirm that chauvinism, in the end, strikes at its own power, weakens its foundations, expands the internal contradictions and may split society with miserable consequences. Illustrations to prove this may be found in the destinies of the Roman, Ottoman, Austro-Hungarian, Prussian, Russian and Soviet Empires.

In the present-day environment small countries and nations

experience the pressure of chauvinistic threats and are inevitably forced to search for a counterbalance to powerful aspirations in order to ensure their security and sovereignty. All this, generally speaking, does not enhance the structure of international relationships and may aggravate contradictions at a global level.

From what has been said above, it follows that for citizens of the Republic of Uzbekistan the vital issues are the extent to which the elements of great-power chauvinism and aggressive nationalism are powerful today in relation to our country and what real dangers to our security this phenomenon offers, whatever appearances it might have.

The year 1991 was an historic turning point: when the former victims of the totalitarian system obtained liberation for their potential for state-national revival. And the natural result was symbolical: Russia started to dismantle its decrepit, weakened and disintegrating Empire. That is why a democratically structured, economically and politically healthy and prosperous Russia is so necessary for strengthening the independence of all new sovereign states, including the Republic of Uzbekistan.

It seemed at first that after the demise of the party of the imperial power, chauvinism would be a thing of the past. But events have proved otherwise.

What are the manifestations of the symbols of great power, based on chauvinism and aggressive nationalism, today? Frank disappointment can be traced in the words and actions of certain politicians and experts at the growing understanding that Moscow and Russia are not the former Soviet Union. This causes irritation and a kind of painful reaction to the fact that in the former Soviet Republics their national-state interests are not only clearly expressed, but that a quite independent policy is being conducted to implement these goals.

Lately, in the Russian press, many analytical materials have been repeatedly published which by their tenor and content reveal the hand of special agencies and politicians, not the hand of a journalist. These publications openly demonstrate and serve as another argument that the danger of chauvinism and its manifestations in relation to the newly independent states in post-Soviet space is not an invented problem, but a threat equally dangerous to Russia and to its neighbors.

In some articles, the frankness and ambitions of the dyed-in-the-wool chauvinists and nationalists exceed all limits. It is enough to take the editorial in the *Novaya Nezavisimaya Gazeta* published on March 26, 1997, titled 'CIS: Beginning or End of History'.

In this article, published on the eve of the meeting of the Heads of the CIS on March 28, 1997, the editor's views on 'the entirely new approaches towards unification in post-Soviet territory' are exposed. Unfortunately, a reading of that article (or 'report' as the anonymous author calls it), obviously shows that there is no way of seeing new approaches to integration. On the contrary, it directly supports (a view absolutely inadmissible from the point of view of international law and the ethical norms of respect for independent and sovereign states – UN-members) an appeal to destabilize the situation in these countries, to revise the present-day *status quo* and realities in post-Soviet territory. And this, in the author's judgement, for the sake of ensuring Russia's security and preserving its dominant position within former USSR borders.

Thus they consider that: 'Russia's biggest mistake is that it actually agreed with such integration logic, under which the former Soviet Republics develop from the stage of proto-state entities to become real states with all relevant attributes, then they implement integration in the economic sphere, and only after that do they implement the process of military and political integration, and the creation of a really renewed union of sovereign and free states.'

As a remedy to correct this mistake 'Russia's resolute involvement in the process of statehood building should be offered in the former Republics of the USSR in order not to allow their using all their economic, military, ethno-demographic and other levers to consolidate their state power around the forces of anti-Russian and anti-integration orientation. Only active measures (destabilization of the internal political situation in the regions . . . included) are able to prevent the process of a slow (but inevitable under the current policy of the Russian authorities) withdrawal of these states from Russia.'

So, as they see it, 'Changes in priorities will give the motive to Russia to revise the whole existing system of agreements on territorial delimitation between the Republics after the fall of the

USSR, to ignore the principle of territorial integrity so far as it applies to them, and to put forward the issue of the repartition of the area on the basis of a nation's right of self-determination.'

The authors of the article are particularly fearful of the strengthening integration of the Central Asian states, considering it an alleged 'threat from the South'. They are convinced that the integration of the Central Asian states 'undermines the interests of the Russian economy in the region, and the course of subordinating post-Soviet state economies to the developed countries of the South and the West leaves no place for Russia'. From this position they give this advice: 'Russia should concentrate its efforts on hindering the union of the Central Asia bloc now during its formation, splitting it and instigating internal regional competition.'

For these purposes, it is proposed to use all possible means and methods to exert influence, ranging from a 'policy of stick' (regulation or threat to regulate the export of raw materials from these states, along with tough conditions for restructuring their external debts to Russia) to a 'policy of carrot' (military, economic and financial aid in the form of credits, supplies, orders, incentives, and so on), and even threats 'to withdraw troops (from Tajikistan) and exert territorial claims'. Central Asia's dependence on the Russian transport infrastructure, which 'makes the new states of the region quite vulnerable to the ghost of economic blockade, in the first place of food and energy', is taken into account.

The authors want brutally and categorically to play the card of champion of the Russian-speaking population's interests in this region: 'We are bound to support not only our compatriots who happen unwillingly to be outside Russia, but also the entire phenomenon of the Russian-speaking world of Central Asia. To help the Russians and Russian-speaking movements (especially the Cossacks as the most radical and mobilized Russian section abroad) and opposition forces of Russian orientation in Central Asia, the lobbyist potential of the Russian Federation's state and private structures must be put in action.'

They believe that by using all means of pressure 'Russia will be able to obtain great concessions from the countries of Central Asia, and possibly achieve a complete transformation of the "political status" of the region that will meet more our [Russian] national interests.' Moreover, they are convinced that 'a permanent pressure aimed at the gradual re-orientation of the Central Asian political regimes towards Russia as the main and exclusive center of power in post-Soviet territory is needed'.

One of the basic reasons for the emergence of such ambitions is the imperial past and the chauvinistic way of thinking which is difficult to overcome for some politicians. Apparently, it is extremely difficult for them to reconcile themselves with the consummated historical fact of the new sovereign states, who define their own future.

It is high time to understand that today every independent country has its own history, particularities, pace of development, and its own future, its own relevant and worthy place in the world community.

It is my conviction that time and history are in our favor, to strengthen our independence and sovereignty. Our new life and the advance of history can not be stopped and reversed. At the same time, we are entitled to live in close and good neighborliness, sharing and solving our common problems, as it is done in the civilized and democratic world.

What foundations do the great power's claims have today – the contents of which, despite the modernized appearances, have not changed in principle?

- Much is made of the idea of Russia being a great power, of the rebirth of Russian national exclusiveness, of the creation of a strong geopolitical space surrounding the great power that claims the role of one of the world's poles.
- There are shameful speculations about the difficulties of the transition to market relations, characteristic all over the post-Soviet territory. Such speculators use a very simple logic, but far from being inoffensive and unselfish they connect the present-day difficulties with the disintegration of the Union, and hence, the restoration of 'a united and friendly family of peoples' would allow them to overcome their difficulties rapidly and efficiently.
- There exists another echo of great power chauvinism. Its

defenders usurp the right to decide what countries from 'the near abroad' would be honored with the invitation to cooperate.

- ◆ Representatives of intellectual sources respected in Russia make arrogant pronouncements on the alleged parasitism of the former Soviet Republics, which, they say, dream even now of subsisting on the account of Moscow.

In talking about the threat of great-power chauvinism and aggressive nationalism, we are essentially implying the danger of:

1. international, interstate and interethnic confrontation;
2. resistance to the realization of our internationally legal and intrastate sovereignty;
3. attempts to restrict Uzbekistan's external economic links and predetermine their unequal character;
4. informational and ideological pressure on the population of our country and the aspiration to perpetuate a distorted image of Uzbekistan in the eyes of world public opinion;
5. provocation of interethnic distrust and aggravation of interethnic relations, assuming that great-power chauvinism and extremist nationalism always go hand in hand;
6. imposition of neo-colonialist and neo-imperial approaches and the breaking-up of mutually beneficial and equal co-operation in all spheres.

Speaking straightforwardly, the state leadership of Russia as a whole began to understand the need for juridical equality within the CIS. We share Boris Yeltsin's opinion that 'the restoration of the former Union will turn out to be a tragedy'. To adhere to such a position is a basic principle of our interstate relationship. Precisely such an approach by Russia's leadership towards the establishment of mutually beneficial and equal relations within the CIS is and will be in the future the foundation of interrelations between Russia and Uzbekistan.

In criticizing great-power chauvinism and aggressive nationalism, we, here in Uzbekistan, stand for the development of new relations within the territory of the former Soviet Union and first and foremost with Russia. We have centuries-old links of friendship, brotherhood and mutual assistance with that country and its great people. In the end, the rejection of imperial thinking in Russia and a demonstration of readiness for co-operation with Uzbekistan will open attractive opportunities for our great neighbor.

1. I would like to focus on the evident truth that to have an independent and strong partner is much cheaper and more reliable than to 'support a younger brother' or to 'retain a minor ally within the framework'. In other words, it is better to deal with a strong and stable partner than with a weak ally.

2. An equal and respectful attitude based on a mutual accounting and a balance of interests will give rise to a positive reaction not only within the political leadership of our country, but within the whole nation. Kind feelings and the benign attitude of the people are probably the major capital which Russian politicians can gain in our region. Contrariwise, the conflict in Chechnya should serve as a vivid reminder of where the situation will lead when people's feelings are expressed with only one word – 'hate'.

3. It is important to understand that the formation of sufficiently stable independent states in the region capable of playing the role of a regional buffer is fully in harmony with Russia's geopolitical interests, and at a lower cost. A stable region constitutes a challenge to neither Russia nor any other state. On the contrary, it implies enormous economic and other horizons and, what is more fundamental, it is a guarantee that the region will never become the site of confrontation between civilizations, but will serve as an example of their intermingling and enrichment. The Republic of Uzbekistan is ready to carry out this noble and historic undertaking to the full.

A growing number of people and sober politicians in Russia share this view of interrelations between our countries. They are aware that the future should be built only on the basis of the consideration of mutual interests, and of equal and mutually beneficial co-operation. All this gives certain hope.

Chapter Four

Ethnic and interethnic contradictions

It is commonly known that modern states can be divided predominantly into two types: polyethnic and monoethnic. It is also known that our planet is inhabited by 1,600 ethnic groups that have their own unique cultural and spiritual values. Such a diversity implies the real richness of the world, and the possibility of exchanging values and mutual enrichment. But inherent in this is also one of the most difficult problems to solve: the vast majority of the peoples inhabiting the world do not have an identity as a national state because of the fact that, on the political map, only around two hundred states may be found. This fact should serve as a warning to the international community: growing ethnic self-awareness will determine the political dynamics of the modern world for the foreseeable future.

The interrelation between the *titular nation*, i.e. the nation that a country is named after, and the ethnic minorities living in such a multinational and multilingual country, constitutes one of the decisive pre-conditions for that country's internal political stability and national security.

As international experience proves, the stability of the internal political situation, national security and the dynamics of the social and economic development of a multinational state depend directly on the political loyalty of the representatives of its non-titular nationalities.

International practice is full of examples of the positive and stimulating influence of the polyethnicity factor on the social-political development of those states where a traditional harmony of interethnic relationships exists. Despite certain interethnic and racial problems, the polyethnicity factor in those countries has not only not constrained their social and economic progress, but, on the contrary, has facilitated it. The intermingling of the nations and cultures in those states has become a good source of spiritual and intellectual enrichment for the peoples living there. Thus, polyethnicity in those states has become an influential tool for the acceleration of democratic reform, for social and economic progress, and for the creation of a civic society.

At the same time, in the history of mankind there are many examples of the opposite kind, where the absence of harmony in interethnic relationships within polyethnic states has led to social and political cataclysms, pushing entire peoples and countries backwards. Here polyethnicity was the most destructive factor with regard to internal political stability and national security not only in separate states, but in many regions.

It is clear that interethnic relationships in a multinational state represent one of the most vital factors relating to national security.

The harmonization of interethnic relationships is of the greatest significance during the period of national consolidation of the newly independent states within post-Soviet territory. These relationships have their roots in the distant past and touch the core of a human being's soul. Problems arising from such relationships are often tortuous and difficult. Unsolved problems of this kind may echo throughout the centuries.

This issue demands a scrupulous and delicate approach and is of particular significance for the Republic of Uzbekistan, which belongs to the polyethnic type of state. In this country along with the titular nation – the Uzbeks – there are representatives of over a hundred nationalities that have their own culture and traditions. Their share of the country's population exceeds 20 per cent.

What are the ethnic and interethnic factors involved in our interactive social processes? To what degree do they threaten security in our particular situation? What ethnic policy is to be pursued in order to preserve stability in Uzbekistan and in the entire Central Asian region?

The modern native peoples who comprise the majority of the population of Central Asia have traveled a complicated and unusual road to nationhood, the roots of which were laid down in the distant past. Despite some controversial phenomena in this domain, an irreversible process of consolidation of national states with a multinational population is under way.

The national diversity in Uzbekistan, in conjunction with the growth of national self-consciousness and the spiritual revival of the Uzbek people, serves as a mighty impulse for the renewal of society and for its democratization, creating favorable conditions for the Republic's integration into the world community.

It is no secret that in the USSR everything *national* was regarded as an obstacle to implementing the ultimate goal of communist ideology: to *internationalize* the population and to implement the idea of the 'center' with the formation of the specific social community of 'Soviet people'.

Advancing this conception, communist ideologists and politicians it seems conscientiously confused the natural processes of the growth of national self-consciousness with an aggressive, politicized nationalism. Thus they pursued the goal of distracting the people from organically growing (owing to objective causes) in national self-consciousness. They made accusations of 'nationalism', and repressed people with progressive views and loyal to their people in the republics and national outlying districts. This was the center maintaining a forced 'internationalization', quashing national particularities, trying to speed up the process of creating a 'multinational' community, and responding to its own imperial interests. Such an artificial process of '*rapprochement* of peoples and nations' facilitated the covert and overt resistance that they were accustomed to name 'nationalism'.

In reality, in our view, we are dealing here with a natural aspiration to preserve the genuine national values, originality and traditions of people along with the need to preserve the nation as a subject of social and historical evolution. In fact any nation, even the smallest one, demonstrates the richness of mankind. The disappearance of any national community with its linguistic, cultural and other distinctive features leads to the impovertishment of the earth's cultural and genetic reserves, and to depersonalization. So, the preservation of every ethnic community should be the most important task for all individuals in that community. And this is the paramount goal of every individual state that is made up of ethnic groups.

The desire of one nation to realize its needs and interests should not be made at the expense of the wishes of any other nation or representatives of other nationalities. It is necessary to eradicate any grounds for an arrogant, scornful attitude in the representatives of one nation and people towards another.

In this connection it should be pointed out that there are often contradictions arising from a mismatch of interests and needs of the ethnic groups and nations in interaction. This interaction may cause extreme manifestations of 'nationalism'. It is also necessary to underline that such a politicized 'nationalism' may have a powerfully negative influence and become a strong threat to state and national, regional and global security.

In the complicated present-day conditions of the transition period, in the solution of problems associated with building a civic society based on the revival of national self-consciousness, peace and interethnic accord, the following realities should be taken into consideration:

1. Certain non-antagonistic contradictions in the domain of inter-ethnic relations are a real challenge during the consolidation period of the newly independent states. National needs and interests can be compatible with the needs and interests of civic democratic society.
2. The existing contradictions should not be allowed to develop into interethnic conflicts with tragic consequences threatening the security of peoples and states.
3. It is necessary to take into account the social and political situation, inequality and the necessity for peoples to live together, sharing their desires and aspirations, which should be expressed through an appropriate ethnopolicy of the state and through the formation of public opinion.

Are there threats to interethnic relations in Uzbekistan and the Central Asian region?

If the situation is evaluated objectively, it is true that conflicts can emerge. They result from the policy pursued by the Russian Empire which the Soviet power continued to pursue concerning the delimitation of the territorial and administrative boundaries of the republics in Central Asia.

Historically in Turkestan there was a mixed distribution of tribes and peoples, characterized by oasis-like settlements and a nomadic way of life of people closely linked by a common religion and culture and related languages.

The deliberate migratory policy first of Tsarist Russia and subsequently of the Soviet state provided the conditions for the increase in polyethnicity among the populations of the Central Asian region. Today the territory of the post-Soviet republics of Central Asia is home to over 120 nations and nationalities. Representatives of almost 20 nations came to be in the region as deportees as a result of Stalinist repression.

The ethno-demographic situation in the region constitutes another threat. Changes in this situation have been constantly taking place in Central Asia. In different periods these changes were influenced by such factors as colonization, the industrialization of the 1920s and 30s, the deportation and forced displacement of peoples, active urbanization processes.

All this has been inherited by the newly independent states. That is why the problems of interethnic and subethnic interactions are of strategic significance and make attention to building up the interstate relationship in the region particularly important.

Nowadays the growing significance of ethnic and interethnic factors in the process of preserving stability in the Central Asian region demands that some principal points should be taken into consideration. The most important among them are, in our view, the following:

1. The recognition of state boundaries and their inviolability should be a constituent principle of the external policy of every state, the main pre-condition for securing sovereignty and strengthening political and economic independence.

2. The development of the national self-consciousness of peoples in the region since 1991 has become an irreversible process. A number of them have already become nations, a significant factor in the process of inter-national relations.
3. The geographical, ethnocultural and social-religious proximity of the peoples inhabiting the region constitutes a positive aspect of interethnic dialogue and provides opportunities for inter-state political and economic relations.
4. Ethnopolitics, implemented in Uzbekistan in particular within the framework of the movement 'Turkestan Is Our Common Home', is in its aims and substance a humane and constructive process because it is aimed at achieving interethnic accord in the region. Undoubtedly, this policy fully serves the strategic state and national interests of all Central Asia. 'Turkestan' historically implies not only peoples of Turkic origin, but the whole population of the area.
5. Integrational processes in the region also are to be promoted on the basis of an optimal combination of state and national interests and those of the entire multinational population.

At the same time any attempts to play one people of Central Asia against another and to disseminate myths on spurious grounds of national superiority must be decisively prevented. Such actions are now being taken by some irresponsible, short-sighted and ambitious politicians both within the region and abroad. Whatever motives lie behind these attempts, they can only seriously undermine civic peace and interethnic accord in the region. Where this may lead is shown by the tragic events in the former Yugoslavia, Nagorny Karabakh and other multinational states. Unfortunately we have also had our own sad experience when several extremist groups openly incited clashes and confrontations of people on ethnic grounds. Fortunately, the common sense, wisdom, humanity and kindness that are so characteristic of the Uzbek people triumphed over the narrow interests of separate groups and served as a powerful shield against extremist manifestations.

It is evident that certain differences in the content and speed of social, political and economic reform taking place in the states of Central Asia may also have a negative impact on the interrelationship between nations and nationalities. This demands the implementation of a well-balanced ethnic policy. It is a great comfort that all the states in the region have adopted mutual obligations aimed at securing the rights of citizens regardless of their nationality and at creating favorable conditions for the development of the national culture of the people living in these countries.

The multinational composition of Uzbekistan predetermines its cultural distinctiveness and rich potential for progress. This potential, from our point of view, is conditioned by:

1. the influence of natural climatic conditions in the region and of historical and cultural experience on the way of living of the people that inhabit it;
2. the proximity of the region to the frontier areas of neighboring states that facilitate the intermingling of cultures and the spread of multilingualism (when the population freely uses several languages);
3. the historically conditioned mode of social and public relations, within a family, an area, a region;
4. a tolerant attitude, characteristic of the indigenous peoples of Central Asia, towards representatives of other nationalities. The Uzbeks, for example, have developed this humane feeling to such an extent that national and spiritual tolerance has become an inalienable feature of their general culture and mentality.

A shining example of the richness of soul, of the kindness and compassion for the misfortune of others, and of the benevolence and hospitality characteristic of the Uzbek people was the warm and caring attitude towards the individuals, families and even entire peoples who found themselves in the land of Uzbekistan during the years of hard trials, wars and Stalinist repression.

There could not be many examples in history of a whole nation demonstrating such highly noble feelings and moral qualities as in those troubled years when the Uzbek people deprived themselves and their children of the most necessary things to share them with complete strangers in great need, and when, in Uzbek families with their many children, dozens of orphan children of different nationalities received parental care and tenderness.

Uzbekistan is proud of the fact that this happened and is now a part of its history. We are proud of the fact that in the historical memory of our people and the state there are no shameful pages of anti-Semitism, racism and other forms of arrogance and disrespect towards another nation, another people.

Evaluating as a whole the advancement of democratic and political reforms in the initial stages of the transition period, we may say that Uzbekistan is implementing a special approach. Our model of statehood building is based on the idea of preserving and consolidating the multinational structure of the society historically formed on our territory and using it to achieve the ultimate objective of creating a democratic state governed by its own laws and its own civic society.

At present, national and other social movements, including youth, cultural and religious movements, are experiencing a rebirth. The transition from the euphoria of the first years of independence to the reality of the present and to a sober evaluation of the economic and political situation makes them radically reconsider their aims, refuse to put forward demands of a radical and uncompromising character, undertake ideological and organizational reconstruction, and overcome populist, purely political and ambitious interests.

The civilized legal foundation which addresses issues of equality for citizens of Uzbekistan helps to preserve interethnic accord in our society, defined by its composition as 'unity in diversity'. The Constitution of the Republic underlines that: 'All citizens of the Republic of Uzbekistan, regardless of their nationality, constitute the people of Uzbekistan.' The Law of the Republic of Uzbekistan *On Guarantees of Citizens' Voting Rights* gives to all citizens of the Republic of Uzbekistan 'regardless of origin, social and property status, race, nationality, sex, education, language, religion and occupation' equal voting rights.

The state conception of the protection of the rights of ethnic minorities in the territory of Uzbekistan is clearly revealed in the Constitution of the Republic which says: 'The Republic of Uzbekistan shall ensure a respectful attitude toward the languages, customs and traditions of all nationalities and ethnic groups living on its territory and create the conditions necessary for their development.'

In this regard it would be useful to point out that the processes of national rebirth are not taking place among the Uzbeks solely. Consolidation processes based on ethnocultural grounds are actively underway also among other nationalities living in the territory of Uzbekistan.

In 1989 social associations, and national and cultural centers were set up. Today there are more than 80 such centers in the Republic. They play a positive role in the process of political, economic, cultural-spiritual reform of our multinational society. When we talk about a people's unity, its cohesion and tranquility, we keep stressing that this is a value that has no price.

Our society fosters good international and interethnic relations which support the ideals of freedom and equality for all people, wherever they might be. The unity of any nation, the Uzbek nation included, implies close relations with its ethnic brothers living in other sovereign states, including the Central Asian countries.

Statistics show that today a considerable number of Uzbeks live outside Uzbekistan. For instance, 24.4 per cent of the total population of Tajikistan are Uzbeks; in Kyrgyzstan the percentage is 13.8 per cent; in Turkmenistan 9.0 per cent; in Kazakhstan 2.5 per cent. That is why Uzbekistan cultivates at all levels interrelations between the sovereign states of Central Asia and solid security in the region. The positive results of integration will contribute to an interethnic dialogue and regional security.

Advancing the conception of interrelationship under the motto 'Turkestan Is Our Common Home', we seek the normalization of human relations both in the region and in individual states.

Finally, let us put a question to ourselves: what basic principles should guide Uzbekistan's national policy in order to avoid situations of conflict that threaten national and regional security in the domain of interethnic relations?

Firstly, the ethnopolicy of the state should be based on the priority of the protection of rights, including the rights of an individual and the rights of national minorities.

Secondly, the strategic thrust of the state's ethnopolicy should be based on measures that are able to solve interethnic conflicts and challenges in a constructive manner.

Thirdly, the economic progress of our society, based on a market economy but with a strong element of social security for the people, should support the interests of all nationalities who live in the Republic and create a solid foundation for the realization of the abilities and talents of each individual and the development and well-being of the family.

Thus, for a state to achieve polyethnicity requires a stage-by-stage promotion of interethnic relations based on the natural links which prevail. This calls for a sustained sociological analysis of these processes with the aim of preventing those ethnic and interethnic conflicts which can constitute a threat to state and regional stability.

Chapter Five

Corruption and criminality

In the history of every state, the transition to a new social polity has, unfortunately, always had in its background such repugnant phenomena as corruption and criminality. And the growth of criminality does not only constitute a serious constraint on the path of reforms, but also, under certain circumstances, poses a direct threat to the achievement of planned objectives during the transitional period.

The Republic of Uzbekistan, as well as other states of Central Asia, in this case is no exception. Problems related to the fight against criminality and corruption provoke an interest that is far from abstract. Of course, it is possible to cite the universally accepted opinion that the complicated period of transition from totalitarianism to democracy and a market economy implies in essence the break-up of fundamental political, economic and cultural structures which has a negative effect on moral and ethical norms and is inevitably accompanied by a growth in criminality and corruption. But it seems that this alone is insufficient to understand fully the threat to the security, stability and ultimately the fledgling independence of our state that these phenomena represent.

Criminal activity, sad as it is to say, has existed in all countries and in all times. However during the transition period its significance extends beyond the patterns of crime. The essence of the reforms that are being implemented in the newly independent states is to a major extent conditioned by the fact that the process of property redistribution really takes place. The essence of such redistribution is that the national wealth usurped by the state under the former regime should belong to those who created it and who contributed to its growth.

Each country individually defines the forms and rates of this process, and tries to safeguard it against the sinister influence of the criminal world. By this, not only such criminal acts as robbery, murder and violence against an individual are implied. During the transition period so-called economic crimes are frequently more dangerous. They are conditioned by the new emerging economic mechanisms when the bulk of the population begins to learn how to survive in the environment of a market economy and to understand its objective laws.

The overt and covert participation of criminal elements in the formation of a new economic system based on free market principles encourages an atmosphere of low morality in society and may lead to the formation of a special type of criminal market economy that is unacceptable both to an individual country and to the world community.

A criminal or, as it is often called, a 'shadow economy' grew up and developed as an illegal phenomenon in the sphere of independent monopolistic production when the activity of the nearest competitors — state-owned economic agencies — was restricted by dogmatic instructions and prohibitions. In the Soviet period this phenomenon developed hypertrophied and ugly forms, which were inherited by Uzbekistan as well.

The criminal 'shadow economy' generates organized crime; those corrupted by it include state officials of various levels and ranks. Corruption springs up and it is related primarily to the opportunities and services provided by the state being used to render direct help to organized criminal structures. This represents a direct threat to the security and stability of society due to the negative consequences that criminality and corruption hold for society.

Every honest citizen who values his country's future and prestige should be aware of that threat. Everybody who wants stable conditions for honest work and the application of his or her knowledge, energy and creative fantasy, everybody who dreams that their children and relatives have the possibility from now on to enjoy to the full the fruits of a civilized market economy in a democratic civic society should have a good understanding of the consequences criminality and corruption may unleash, if they are not speedily counteracted.

Historical experience and present-day practice, including that of the newly independent states, make it possible to identify clearly the threats to security which criminality and corruption bring about.

Firstly, at a political level corruption implies an explicit resistance to the ongoing reforms and objectively combines the interests of the obsolete administrative-command system and the 'shadow economy' that try to impede the promotion of new economic relationships and create a potential threat to their existence. Their goal is personal enrichment and their kinsfolk's interests stand above the state's interests; corrupt officials inflict irreparable damage to the political and economic course of the country and the overwhelming majority of the population. Moreover, during the transition period, when the foundations of the new economic order are laid down and a qualitatively different political system is adopted, corruption is able to block this process.

Secondly, crime and corruption scandals erode the constitutional bases of the state and lead to serious violations of human rights and freedoms. There is an absolutely vicious principle that says that 'laws and rules are adopted in order to be avoided' and the result is that society loses its capacity to maintain elementary legal and social order. What sort of sustainability and stability in society can we speak of, if the economy 'is ruled over' by criminal groups and gangs, and people walk the streets in fear?

Thirdly, crime and corruption undermine the moral basis of society, disorient the civic standing of its members, create prerequisites for the formation of a negative attitude towards the ongoing transformations, discredit the very idea of reforms and cause a nostalgic feeling for the 'hard hand of the omnipotent center'.

During the transitional period, characterized by unavoidable losses and hardships for citizens, particularly the younger generation, there may be created and consolidated a deeply amoral position which stipulates that the basic means to achieve higher living standards is connected with unlawful actions. The aspiration to get rich quickly and easily, when social and legal controls do not deal properly with these violations, spoils people, especially the young, who are beginning their independent life. Is there anything more fatal for a state and a society than the seduction and loss of a whole generation?

Fourthly, there is the widely held opinion that 'the roots of money reach out for power'. But if wealth has been acquired through crime, it is easy to imagine what kind of management methods moneyholders will resort to, if they come to administer the power structures of society.

The method of gaining power by criminal groups is well known and proved in many countries. Initially, it is the establishment and consolidation of links within the authority structures to keep safe and further to use the sources from which illegal earnings come, and later on to use the power itself.

The criminalization of government agencies constitutes one of the major threats for a society during its development. The merging of criminal groups and state officials, and their penetration into different branches of power strengthens citizens' feelings of defencelessness and compromises the state in their eyes, which is discredited both within the country and outside.

Fifthly, it is necessary to realized that those who gained their wealth in a dishonest way are ready for any actions to avoid punishment and protect their criminal capital. Such people fear just punishment and are ready to employ all means, right up to the destabilization of society and the organization of mass disorder. There is nothing more agreeable to them than to stir up emotions, incite a crowd and hide behind it. The credo of such people – 'Après nous, le déluge' – is an extreme manifestation of egoism and of disregard for their co-citizens.

Sixthly, there are many examples everywhere, including in our country, that reveal the desire of people who have accumulated their wealth through crime and managed to 'launder dirty money' to burst into politics under the title of newly emerged dissidents, human rights' champions and even victimized fighters for democracy.

Is it worth repeating once more that these actions seriously damage such noble human ideals as justice and democracy, casting a shadow over their nation and their country. As a matter of fact, they are profoundly indifferent to the fate of their own people and country, and their ideals of freedom and independence.

The conduct of such people is a chain of criminal actions: to accumulate capital by defrauding their own nation, to gain political capital by juggling public opinion, to gamble with the values of democracy and justice. It is no secret that these sorts of people are always ready to serve those external forces that try to exert an influence on the situation in the Republic to suit their own interests. So the logical question is: what kind of deceit will they resort to next time?

Seventhly, the activities of corrupt officials during the processes of implementing such priority goals for Uzbekistan as integration in the framework of world economic links and a targeted activity to attract foreign investors and businessmen to the ongoing economic reforms not only drive the honest citizens of our country far from entrepreneurship, but also undermine the confidence of foreign partners.

All this results in the country's loss of vitally important sources of investment, technology and experience and the loss of the possibility for integration in the healthy, 'clean' part of the world economic system. The country becomes more and more an object of interest for international shadow and criminal structures.

It is no less dangerous that in the modern criminal environment, which is becoming more organized and professionally shaped, the trends towards the consolidation of criminal communities, the monopolization of consumer markets by criminal groups, the legalization of illegally gained capital through economic and commercial entities are very easily traced.

Undoubtedly in Uzbekistan measures are being taken to unmask and reveal the causes of criminality, and corrupt officials found guilty are punished severely. Domestic criminality will always be a focus of state attention. In order to prevent the raging escalation of crime and the exploitation of authority by corrupt state officials, a comprehensive set of long-term measures which define our strategy to fight crime has been enacted.

In the framework of this strategy, what guidelines are preferred and need the understanding and support of our society?

First of all, economic measures are necessary. The very logic of fighting against crime and corruption urges further steady progress in the liberalization of economic relations, providing genuine freedom for fair entrepreneurship, removing the remaining sometimes numerous bureaucratic barriers in its way.

The program designed to update the legal and judicial system in Uzbekistan should be regarded as a powerful counteraction to domestic crime and corruption. The legal and judicial system should ensure the absolute rule of law and the guaranteed protection of a citizen's rights. On the other hand, there is an urgent need to radically improve the level of legal education in the country's population, particularly its youth.

The best protection from the corrosion of society which criminality and corruption cause is an inner immunity to criminal offences and a high morality in our citizens. The moral education in a family, school, labour collective or *mahalla*, the moral authority of public opinion, the mass media and the clergy – all these are essential for building a strong awareness among the people of the undesirability of violations of the law.

Finally, it is very important to create an atmosphere of intolerance towards and general disapproval of crime and corruption. The corrupt criminal world fears most of all the public disapproval of its actions. So we anticipate that the further liberalization of our press and other mass media will contribute considerably to the program of fighting against crime.

While analyzing such a complex phenomenon as criminality, we must keep in mind another aspect of this problem. It may be expressed succinctly in one maxim: *a criminal world disregards frontiers.*

International experience provides many examples of the dream of easy and large fortunes uniting criminal elements from various countries, making them into international criminal associations. They are active wherever there is the possibility of acquiring dirty money.

1. There is the *production of drugs and drug trafficking.* The opportunities to obtain the huge profits which this criminal business provides encourages its performers to expand their operations,

disregarding the norms of international law, national legislation and the fatal consequences that 'white death' brings about.

2. There is *arms smuggling*. This 'business' is also very profitable for those who try 'to catch fish in the troubled waters' of regional conflicts and local wars. It is strange to repeat once more that the continuation of armed clashes and the maintenance of tension serve as the best conditions for the expansion of the black market for arms dealers.

Arms smuggling gives birth to such criminal actions as international terrorism. Obviously there is still a lot of time to pass before the desire to earn money out of other people's blood disappears. Is there any need to say that for such 'businessmen' money obtained from bloodshed and dirty politics is the best tool to instigate conflicts in other parts of the world, and to recruit and train international gangsters?

3. There is one more type of international crime which emerged especially following the break-up of the USSR. It is the desire of some regimes and organizations to gain access to nuclear energy sources and the technology of dual (energy and weapon) utilization. It is terrifying to imagine the consequences of technology designed for the production of weapons of mass destruction falling into the hands of political or simply criminal maniacs.

All these categories of international crime not only pose a real threat to an individual country, but they also jeopardize the prospects for maintaining global security. We, the people of Uzbekistan, are perfectly aware that, from this point of view, the Central Asian region is considered to be a dainty piece of pie by international criminal groups. The region is located at the crossroads of international communication links and nobody can guarantee that this advantage will not be used by drug traffickers. The region continues to be the scene of bloody conflicts and so much weaponry is stored here that it has become highly tempting for arms smugglers and for those who regard Central Asia as a training facility for international terrorists. The region also has considerable resources of substances with nuclear fission properties; there are high technology industries, including those of the dual utilization. All this undoubtedly incites the interest not only of honest businessmen, but also of criminal syndicates as well.

So criminality and corruption are sources of real threat both to national and international security. The consequence of this is that the problems of crime prevention are not only addressed to us. That is why we believe that crime is the concern of the whole international community. The people and the leadership of sovereign Uzbekistan are ready to co-operate and consider it as their contribution to clean the world and provide its security.

Chapter Six

Regionalism and clans

Most dictionaries define the word 'clan' as a phenomenon characteristic of feudal society. A clan is a community of people united by blood and kinship links. Clans were given the name of their heads, who were the highest authority for their members and represented their members' interests outside the confines of the relatively closed life of a tribal community. It was the clan that defended its members, providing for them protection and assistance.

Over time, new social and economic formations emerged and, in consequence, relationships among people have changed as well. But although the relationships have changed, they have not disappeared completely. Just as the fossil remains of a dead plant may sometimes be discovered in a rock, so in modern society and its social and cultural characteristics there is a clear trace of the distant past. This is what has happened to clans.

In the present-day world it is hardly possible to find a society with a traditional and classic clan division. But sometimes it presents itself in a modified, 'modernized' form. In many countries blood relations are not as strong as they were. However, they have been replaced by links of another community, another identity including territorial and national groups. It seems that there is nothing wrong with descendants of this or that local area who have settled down elsewhere, in another part of the country, helping their fellow kinsmen.

It seems quite natural for people to provide mutual aid to each other when they are related to some extent by kinship. But when, through groups based on kinship, regional or ethnic principles are developed (mostly informal) in governmental or other structures, prompted by their narrow interests, and these groups promote their interests over the interests of the state to the detriment of the common cause and nationwide interests; when in order to achieve their goals such groups plan to move up their members into the existing state power or other sorts of hierarchy, then it becomes dangerous.

We have to speak about regionalism and clan influence causing a real threat to the stability and security of society. At present, there is no serious or profound analysis of these phenomena. They must not be considered as a characteristic feature exclusive to underdeveloped countries or countries in their transitional period. Some economically developed Western countries are also susceptible to them. Regionalism and clan influence are the signs of a narrow, ethno-regional type of mentality, which reduces the diversity, complexity and interrelationship of the world to the size of one area, one people, one large expanded family.

What are the reasons for the vitality of such phenomena and their continuous reproduction in the existing surroundings, and how are they revealed in our environment?

Clan and countrymen groups in government structures are formed on an ethnic basis. The ultimate goal of a clan is to push its members as far as possible up into the ranks of the state hierarchy. The feature which distinguishes members of a clan is the same birthplace. This is important: it is not shared professional skills, nor a shared world outlook, nor shared spiritual interests, but simply a shared birthplace.

So, regional self-consciousness, in other words people's perception of themselves exclusively in terms of the place where they were born and grew up, in fact provides the essential ethno-social basis for regionalism and clan influence. Obviously, there are still serious grounds for stating that in some parts of Central Asia regional self-awareness outstrips national self-awareness.

It should be noted that this situation is largely typical of peoples who are in the process of ethnic consolidation, when the essential features and characteristics of the ultimate form of ethnic unity, a nation, are being shaped.

An analysis of the ethno-social situation in some countries reveals that ethnic diversity exists when separate groups within one nation are distinguished from each other not only in their dialect, but also in their economic and cultural organization. This creates the conditions for regionalism and clan influence.

Historically Central Asia has no tradition of building statehood on the basis of national criteria. All the states that existed in the region before Russian colonization were established mainly on the basis of dynastic or territorial principles (Khanates of Bukhara, Kokand and Khiva). It is characteristic that by the time the latter Khanates were established, numerous settled and nomadic tribes were living in the area where there had previously been centralized states and empires.

The disconnection of one nation, its division into several Khanates — accompanied by ruinous wars — reinforced and retained feudal separation right up to the Soviet period.

The establishment of Soviet power in the region, its striving for 'internationalisation' and standardization of all national features led to a situation where the differences between the ethnic communities, and even within one nation between different groups, did not disappear but obtained new impetus.

It was precisely state socialism with its typically rigid planned economy, state-owned property and centralized distribution of benefits that created fertile soil for the existence and full-scale expansion of regionalism and clan influence.

In the USSR clan influence and regionalism acquired a quality of another kind. The rigidity and sometimes severity of the centrally planned economy and the state-ownership of property became fertile soil. Managers and administrators of various levels and ranks were the actual distributors of material and other kinds of benefits. That is why the local authorities and heads of economic sectors, enterprises and trading establishments were in pursuit of their patronage.

A personal recommendation by the acquaintance of an official or closely related person to him — a relative, a friend, a countryman — was the magic word that opened the doors of his office. In his turn, such an administrator needed a reliable and loyal environment to maintain and reinforce his position in power. The principle of personal loyalty became one of the criteria of his staff selection policy. The leitmotiv of this policy is the words of one of the characters from Russian literature: 'Why not take care of our own dear little man?'

This system of relations in society, where the interests of a separate group of people or of separate areas dominate the common interest, is extremely corrupt and dangerous. It results in social tensions in society and poses a threat to the state – to its stability, integrity and capacity for progress. During the Soviet period, when all sorts of fantastic ideas held sway, there were various conflicts caused by the rival interests of opposing clans. These were traditionally solved by using powerful repressive machinery, while the propaganda machine screened everything behind a thick veil of silence.

Striving for the elimination of such a corrupt legacy is one of the primary strategic tasks of our state. Necessary prerequisites grew up and gained strength when independence became a reality. That is why it is a priority of the highest political importance to urge the need energetically to cut short regionalism and the formation of cliques which are hampering our common cause. We must continue to emphasize that there is only one Uzbek nation in the world, and there are no national differences between the descendants of Khorezm, Ferghana, or Surkhandarya: they are all Uzbeks.

The most dangerous delusion is to elevate territorial differences to an absolute. It is not regional self-consciousness that ought to determine the national self-identification of an individual: a person must, first and foremost, perceive himself as a citizen of Uzbekistan, and only then as an inhabitant of Khorezm, Samarkand or the Ferghana valley. This in no way lessens the significance of our individual 'native areas' – the locality and region where each person was born and grew up – or the particularity of their way of life and system of values. However, it should be borne in mind that an exaggerated local patriotism and its aggressive advancement impede the consolidation of the nation, inevitably lead to internal separatism and cultural isolation, and give rise to a series of other threats to the stability and security of state and society.

What dangers do these phenomena entail? What negative consequences may they lead to? All these are not idle questions for our young independence; the answers to these questions will, to a great extent, determine the destiny of our country's citizens.

First and foremost, the growth of regional tendencies may lead to the self-isolation of the regions, the weakening and break-up of economic links, and, consequently, to the economic decline of a region. This, in turn, can only impair the national economy. Frequently, it is accompanied by the emergence and rapid growth of centrifugal forces inside the state.

Separatist trends in the regions pose a real threat to the integrity of the state. In seeking a dominant position and trying to achieve egoistic goals, a clan or a region may become a breeding ground for different formations pretending to play a nationwide role of political opposition in the framework of the entire state. The struggle for power between such groups expressing itself in extremist forms also poses a direct threat to the territorial integrity of the state and to its very existence.

Political organizations, including those in opposition, should develop within national patterns of society. This will serve as a guarantee that the leaders and members of such organizations regard as of paramount importance the interests of the whole state and nation, and not just the part of them to which they belong because of their origin.

Another potential danger of regionalism and separatism is the risk of interethnic conflicts caused by local and clan contradictions. People of Central Asia's indigenous nations inhabit all five states of the region. The population of these states is predominantly composed of the same ethnic groups (Uzbeks, Kazakhs, Tajiks, Kyrgyzes, Turkmens, Karakalpaks, Uyghurs and others) in varying proportions. In each of the Republics there are areas where people of one or other non-titular nation prevail; for example the Uzbek areas in Kazakhstan, in the southern part of the Osh Region of Kyrgyzstan, in the Leninabad region of Tajikistan, in the Dashaus region of Turkmenistan; the large Kazakh settlements in Tashkent and the Jizzak region; the predominantly Russian areas in the northern part of Kazakhstan, and so forth.

During the complicated period of radical social transformation, national minorities may feel frustrated and uncertain about their future in a particular country. And if these feelings have been formed against a backdrop of growing regionalism and interclan conflict, which have resulted in increasing discrimination in economic and political spheres, then the risk of acute interethnic tension grows sharply, eventually to the point of uncontrolled disturbances and violence. Recent history can show many examples of conflicts and tragic events that have emerged for such reasons in post-Soviet territory.

As for the threats that are posed by regionalism and interclan conflict it is necessary to bear in mind that these phenomena are destructive in their nature; but history has many precedents of external forces using these levers to achieve their own geopolitical goals and mercenary interests against states that are weakened for different reasons.

History also shows that clan leaders and champions of local interests, who seek to use external forces for their own sake, end up becoming not only hostages to the will of these external forces, but also victims who are readily sacrificed by them for justifying their frequently specious actions.

An awareness of the complexity and topicality of this problem, along with a clear idea of what can be done to avoid the formation of a dangerous critical mass, will prevent the conversion of regionalism and clan influence from potential risk to real threat.

The principle of proclaiming the priority of universal human values, of the national interests of Uzbekistan and of the nationwide laws governing the entire territory of the country should be at the core of the work by present-day and future politicians. A recognized unity of corporate (businessmen, intelligentsia, persons related to agriculture, etc.) nationwide interests, but not their kinship-based, territorial or ethnic affiliation, should become the foundation for the organizational consolidation of the individuals in our society.

A balance of interests in all regions, and of all ethnic and social groups, should be constantly sought. A legitimate mechanism for promoting and implementing this balance will act as a barrier to block the emergence and expansion of selfish interests.

The policy of cadres selection in the state distribution sector, which is still existing during this transition period of economic, social and regional policy, should ensure equal possibilities for access to and use of state-owned resources to all areas, all national and social minorities.

Local authorities need greater independence. Knowledge of the specific features of their region enables their officials to maximize material and human resources and to improve the implementation of existing reforms by taking account of local economic, demographic and other peculiarities. To charge local authorities with a significant level of responsibility for the reforms will engage their initiative to the full and allow local resources to be incorporated.

At the same time, greater independence of economic entities and local governments must be combined with a higher personal responsibility of managers and officials to achieve an increase in local budgets, and to discover the most feasible solutions to local economic and social problems. However, unconditional recognition of the priority of national interests should be the basis for such regionalism.

Extending democratic reform and reinforcing the supremacy of universal human values in people's consciousness in society as a whole (a scrupulous work), and struggling with the problems caused by those who espouse ethnic and national self-isolation, are primary conditions for securing the national independence, sovereignty and stability of Uzbekistan, and for averting the danger of regionalism and clan-influence.

To attach the significance of nationwide policy to the spiritual development and enlightenment of the nation and the people. To secure a dialectic combination of national pride and respect for the history, culture and dignity of other nations. To educate and continuously strengthen in society's consciousness the feeling of complicity in and responsibility for all that is happening in the modern world. To educate the young and future generations in a spirit of understanding and awareness of the necessity to assimilate fully the achievements of world history and culture along with a thorough knowledge of the history of their own state and people. — All these are absolutely indispensable conditions if we are to face our future with confidence and rest easy for our children's fate and well-being.

Chapter Seven

Ecological problems

In examining potential threats to national security, the problems of ecological safety and environmental protection deserve special attention. We have to admit frankly that there was no serious consideration of these problems under the previous administrative-command system. This issue was predominantly a subject for investigation by individual researchers and 'a cry from the heart' by concerned individuals who were greatly worried about their country's future and the preservation of its natural wealth.

But their appeals to conscience, civic responsibility and reason encountered a cold, and even cynical indifference on the part of bureaucratic officials of the party and of the Soviet system. There is nothing surprising about this. The very essence of the socialist economic system, based on the predatory exploitation of natural and mineral raw material resources, generating enormous expenditures and losses, was alien to a conserving attitude towards the huge richness available in the country. On the contrary, that was its major trump card in the economic competition of two systems, the basis of its export potential.

The emphasis was put on the extensive development of the economy. In such conditions there could be no discussion about the observance of certain norms and rules regulating the rational use of resources that would guarantee the protection of nature and the environment. Meagre funding was allocated to environmental protection measures, which were not enough to cover a fraction of the damage to nature. Forests were cut in an unreasonable, predatory manner. Huge quantities of fuel and raw mineral resources, far in excess of demand, were extracted and a considerable proportion of them went unprocessed to stockpiles. Industrial giants were constructed with no elementary waste treatment facilities. This resulted in the contamination of vast areas of ground, air and water by toxic and polluting industrial waste and residues. The implementation of large-scale hydrotechnical projects and the construction of transportation communications, including the Baikal-Amur railroad, the Turkestan-Siberian railroad, roads, oil and gas pipelines, and irrigation systems, was the main cause of the exhaustion of natural resources, and has led to the disappearance of entire settlements, damaged the ecological balance, changed the climate and affected people's living and working conditions.

This problem has become more acute in recent years. As a result of the chaotic transition of some of the CIS countries to a market economy, and the loss of management and control of the overuse of natural and raw material resources, they began to be plundered, extracted predatorily and exported at low prices, and turned out to be a source of super-profits for individual 'nouveaux riches' and for entire corrupt groups, who sacrifice the ecological safety and the health and wealth of present and the future generations for their greedy interests. Shamelessly, huge material resources, a unique patrimony of mankind, are being plundered and exterminated, causing enormous damage to the whole environment and affecting the climate; and, what is more important, the natural conditions of life and activity for successive generations are being deformed.

At the meeting point of two centuries, mankind and the population of our country face a global ecological threat. To stand idly by, to be impartial, means to be condemned to extinction. Unfortunately, there are a lot of people who are too careless, too irresponsible about this problem.

The problem of ecological security long ago surpassed national and regional limits and became a global problem for mankind. Nature and man interact on the basis of certain laws; infringement of these laws leads to irreversible ecological disasters.

An understanding of this was reached rather late in the day, not until the beginning of the seventies when this issue was highlighted in the first Western models of global evolution, which produced a 'bomb explosion' effect. Mankind has now become aware of the kind of threat it faces, and of the implications of man-made influences on the environment.

Man's intensive economic activity, disregarding nature and its laws, has led, as one of the studies of the Club of Rome 'The Road into the Twenty-first Century' points out, to all the disasters on the earth: soil erosion, deforestation, the extinction of fish, acid rain, air pollution, the depletion of the ozone layer. Specialists forecast that by the year 2000 the area covered by forest will constitute only one-sixth of the land area, whereas in the fifties it was a quarter. The world's ocean water is disastrously polluted and its reproductive capacity is sharply declining. Accelerated rates of urbanization have caused major urban agglomerations which have become major centers of contamination. The amount of acid rain containing sulfur dioxide and nitrogen oxide has increased. Subsequently, the number of diseases on the globe has risen due to environmental deterioration.

Today, owing to accelerated scientific and technical progress all over the world, the amount of natural resources that is involved in manufacturing processes is increasing. Moreover, the world's annual population growth means that more food, clothing and fuel are required. These are the reasons for the rapid reduction of forest areas, the expansion of deserts, soil deterioration, the depletion of the ozone screen in the upper atmospheric layers, and the increase in average air temperature.

A major threat for the human environment is posed by the unlimited arms race and the production, storage and testing of nuclear, chemical and other weapons of mass destruction.

Today, on the eve of the twenty-first century, amid conditions of rapid scientific and technical progress and changes in the geopolitical structure of the world, the problems of regulating man's influence on the biosphere and of achieving harmony between social progress and the conservation of a favorable natural environment, in short a balanced interrelationship between man and nature, are becoming more acute.

The international community long ago recognized the status and inviolability of a human being's rights not only for life, but also for the normal environmental conditions that are necessary for an adequate and healthy way of living.

Because of its importance and implications for the present and future of human society, ecological security is one of the top priority issues. A constructive solution to such problems will enlarge the quality of life of the present and future generations, and provide the ecologically safe technological development of the industrial sectors of the economy. It is known that the deterioration of the environment does not happen at once, it is a long lasting process and ecological danger is accumulating gradually.

Ecological problems have become one of the most acute global issues of our times; their solution has a bearing on the interests of all people, and will impact, to a great extent, on present and future civilizations. The solution of the extensive problems arising from man's interaction with nature cannot be limited to the context of one country; the problems must be solved within the scope of the entire planet. It is evident that many of the problems associated with the protection of man's environment against the damaging influence of economic activity are of global character, and so may be solved only on the basis of international co-operation. The issue of ecology is a topical one in all countries of the world, in all parts of the earth; the degree of its acuteness varies from country to country and from world region to world region.

We must regretfully say that the Central Asian region represents one of the most dangerous areas of ecological disaster. The cumulative result of having ignored this problem over many decades underlines the complexity of the situation. Practically all spheres of human habitat and activity in the region are jeopardized by the risk of ecological disaster. We have learned to our cost that nature does not tolerate presumptuous mistreatment. Nature forgives nothing. The false dogma of socialist ideology stipulating that man is master of nature has turned out to be, particularly in the Central Asian region, a tragedy for many people. It has put entire populations and nations on the brink of extinction, and of the disappearance of their unique genetic make-up.

Uzbekistan itself has not escaped the influence of these processes. According to some researchers, an extremely complicated and even dangerous situation exists in this country. What does it consist of?

Firstly, the threat of a scarcity of usable land and its low quality is an increasing cause of concern. In Central Asia land is an invaluable treasure: it literally feeds, clothes and creates a material basis for the well-being not only of families directly related to agricultural production, but also of the entire population of the Republic where all branches of the economy are closely linked with the land, and benefit from its generous fruits. At the same time land is not only an enormous patrimony, but also a factor affecting the country's future. This is particularly relevant for Uzbekistan where economic and demographic pressure on the land is growing year by year.

A particular feature of the Republic is that arable land accounts for only 10 per cent of the total area of 447,400 square kilometers. A considerable part of Uzbekistan's territory is covered by deserts and semideserts: Karakum, Kyzylkum, Ustyurt and others. Today the demographic pressure on land, particularly on agricultural land, is extremely high. Among the Central Asian countries Uzbekistan has the highest population density – 51.4 inhabitants per square kilometer, as opposed to 6.1 in Kazakhstan, 22.7 in Kyrgyzstan and 9.4 in Turkmenistan. In the Republic there are 0.17 hectares of arable land per capita, while in Kazakhstan there are 1.54, in Kyrgyzstan 0.26, in the Ukraine 0.59, and in Russia 0.67. Given that more than half of the population live in rural areas, we may definitely state that there is already not just a relative, but an absolute excess of labor resources.

Taking into account the relatively high population growth rate, the accelerated urbanization process and the allocation of fertile land for urban development, housing construction, the creation of new enterprises, and engineering and transportation networks, then in the short term, already on the eve of the twenty-first century, the problem of the availability of land resources will become more acute.

This problem is also aggravated because alongside the process of natural desert expansion, the process of man-made desertification is actively underway. Deterioration of the natural environment is accompanied in this case by land erosion, soil salinization, the disturbance in the levels of surface and undersoil water levels.

Wind and water erosion have a negative effect on soil productivity due to insufficient anti-erosion measures being taken. Measures in the past have been poorly implemented and at a very slow rate, and at the end of the eighties they were practically stopped. Over 2 million hectares, accounting for almost half the total irrigated area, are endangered by this slowing down.

The high degree of land salinization has become a major ecological problem for Uzbekistan. It was caused by the massive land development when large tracts of salinated soil and areas unsuitable for irrigation were put into use for mass cultivation. Over the past 50 years the area of irrigated land has grown from 2.46 million hectares to 4.28 million. During the period of 1975–85 about 1 million hectares of new land were brought under cultivation. By 1990 the area of irrigated land had grown by 50 per cent compared with the 1985 level.

Until recently (1990), cotton accounted for 75 per cent of arable land use. No country in the world has had such a high degree of cotton monocropping and this has led to the destruction of the land, a decrease in soil fertility, a deterioration in the aqueous-physical properties of the soil, a growth of soil deterioration and erosion.

The level of non-organic mineral fertilizers, herbicides and pesticides used in Uzbekistan was far in excess of every set norm. These contaminated soils, rivers, lakes, subsoil water and clean water reserves. Moreover, in the exploitation of new land vital techniques were not observed; excessive, unchecked cotton irrigation and the resulting overmoisture of the soil led to secondary salinization processes.

Large-scale soil pollution with various kinds of industrial and communal waste has become another real threat. Violations of rules for the storage, utilization, transportation and application of chemicals, dangerous substances and mineral fertilizers, and industrial and building materials lead to land pollution and reduce its potential for productive use.

The intensive extraction of mineral resources, often employing outdated processing technology, involves the cumulation of huge amounts of residues, cinder, slag and other substances which not only occupy areas suitable for agricultural purposes, but also cause the contamination of atmospheric air, and surface and subsoil waters, as well as soil pollution. The industry for toxic waste processing has not yet been created.

In the territory of Uzbekistan there are over 230 urban and rural stockpiling zones of solid communal waste amounting to approximately 30 million cubic meters. These were situated randomly without the prior study of geographical, geological, hydrogeological and other conditions. They use rudimentary techniques for decontaminating and burying solid consumer waste. The most complicated waste situation is in the big cities of the Republic. Here there is still no industrial solution to communal waste processing. The country's sole experimental plant for the recycling of waste in Tashkent was put into operation only in 1991.

Radioactive contamination causes a particular danger. From 1944–67 uranium ore processing residues were buried along the river Mayluu-Suu (Kyrgyzstan) and today there are 23 storages that require the construction of dikes and dams, and works aimed at providing protection against land slides and ensuring slope stability in these zones. These storages are ecologically dangerous zones in the Navoi region. There are also radioactive sands which cause a threat because of their displacement by the wind.

As a result of all this, the recovery of the land and the implementation of a broad set of measures targeting a reduction in polluted soil is a task of paramount importance in the environmental protection of Uzbekistan. Radical improvement in the use of natural resources is the main task of the day.

Secondly, the acute shortage of water resources and their contamination, both surface and underground, cause great anxiety in Uzbekistan from the point of view of ecological security. Rivers, canals and water reservoirs of the Republic and even underground waters are subjected to various man-made effects.

In arid areas water is an invaluable gift of nature. All of life depends on water: life comes to a halt where water has gone.

Yet water resources in Central Asia are extremely limited. The major waterways are the Amu-Darya river with an annual capacity of 78 cubic kilometers and the Syr-Darya river with 36 cubic kilometers.

Nowadays all the water resources of the Aral Sea basin are fully consumed by the national economy.

As the watershed is mostly located in the mountains of Kyrgyzstan and Tajikistan, and most water resources are used for irrigation by all Central Asian republics, the problem of the joint and co-ordinated management of the limited water resources of the Aral Sea basin in the interests of all the states of the region and in line with ecological requirements to provide water to the rivers' delta and the Aral Sea in order to create acceptable living conditions there is acute and demands a constructive solution.

Another important problem of the region is connected with the need to implement a set of measures aimed at water protection and water saving through closer linkage of the irrigation network performance with irrigation techniques in order to minimize losses of water. It will be necessary to regulate the flowing of collector-drainage waters and to stop completely the residual waters flowing to the rivers and reservoirs.

The quality of water resources is one of the most important issues. Since the sixties the quality of water in the rivers' basin has increasingly deteriorated due to the large-scale development of new land, the extensive development of industry, cattle-breeding complexes, urbanization, the construction of collector-drainage systems in Central Asia and the ever-increasing intake of river water for irrigation.

Contamination of river water impacts negatively on the hygienic-ecological and sanitary-epidemiological situation, particularly in the estuary areas. On the other hand, the salt content in the tidal waters increases the salination of soil in the delta area of the Amu-Darya, the Syr-Darya, the Zarafshan and other rivers and thus demands additional improvement works, watering operations and the construction of drainage systems.

Of particular significance for Uzbekistan and neighboring regions is the supply to the population of drinking water of adequate quality. Despite the fact that the indices of settlements with standard water supply over only the last five years has increased by approximately 50 per cent, this problem still remains acute, especially if we take into account the fact that contamination of the drinking water supply is the reason for the high level of diseases in the Republic, particularly in areas close to the Aral Sea.

Thirdly, the disappearance of the Aral Sea has become the most acute ecological problem, and a national disaster. The roots of the Aral Sea problem date back far into the past, but the scope of it has expanded over the last decades. The intensive construction of irrigation systems all over the territory of Central Asia, apart from giving water to many settlements and industrial sites, was the cause of a global catastrophe: the drying out of the Aral Sea. Not long ago triumphant trumpets celebrated the increase in new irrigated land reclaimed from deserts. This irrigation water was taken from the Aral, and it was 'forgotten' that this was 'drained blood' from this sea. Today, the Aral Sea area is a zone of ecological disaster.

The Aral crisis is one of the biggest ecological and human catastrophes in recorded history and affects approximately 35 million people who live in the sea basin. Over a 20–25 year period we are witnessing the disappearance of one of the biggest exclusive water reservoirs in the world. Never before has such a case been witnessed in history: in the lifetime of only one generation, the death of a whole sea. Between 1911 and 1962 the Aral Sea level had an absolute mark of 53.4 meters, the volume of water was 1,064 cubic kilometers, with a surface area of 66 thousand square kilometers and water mineralization of 10-11 g/l. The sea had great transport, fishing and climatic significance. The annual supply of water through the Syr-Darya and the Amu-Darya was nearly 56 cubic kilometers.

By 1994 the level had fallen to 32.5 meters, the volume of water was less than 400 cubic kilometers and the water surface had shrunk to 32.3 thousand square kilometers with double the level of mineralization. The result of a 20-meter drop in level is that the Aral is not a single sea any longer, but two lakes. Its shore line has receded by 60–80 kilometers. The Amu-Darya and the Syr-Darya deltas are being increasingly destroyed. The dried seabed now covers an area of more than 4 million hectares. In place of the sea, one more man-made desert of sands and *solonchaks* (salt flats) has come into existence. The winds lift salt and sand from the dried seabed and blow them hundreds of kilometers.

Sandy storms on the dried seabed of the Aral were detected for the first time in 1975 as a result of space surveys. Since the beginning of the eighties such storms have been recorded here 90 days a year. Bands of dust are sometimes 400 kilometers long and 40 kilometers wide, while the area they cover can be up to 300 kilometers in radius. Researchers estimate that between 15 and 75 million tons of dust are lifted into the atmosphere here.

All this has resulted in changes to the climate of the Aral zone. Since 1983 the Aral has ceased being a fishery zone. The rusted frames of the once powerful fishing fleet may now be seen far away from the present-day shore line; fishermen's settlements are destroyed. The bays of Bozkol, Altynkol and Karatma have disappeared; the Akpetkin archipelago has merged with the land. Pastures and meadows are disappearing, the area is bogged up. The increased water shortage and the deterioration in its quality has led to the destruction of soil and vegetation, to changes in flora and fauna, and to a deterioration in the efficiency of irrigated agriculture.

The Aral Sea's drying out and the subsequent degradation of the environment in the Aral zone is defined as an ecological catastrophe. Dust and salt storms, the desertification of land over vast areas not only in the Aral Sea zone but also far from the sea, the changes of climate and landscape are just some of the catastrophic consequences. The Aral catastrophe could have been managed at the beginning of the seventies, or even later at the very beginning of the eighties, when the sea level dropped significantly. Nowadays, management is extremely difficult, and will become more complicated or even impossible. The drying out of the Aral Sea unleashed in the Aral zone a complicated set of ecological, social, economic and demographic problems, the origin and scale of which have global implications. The ecological disaster originated by the drying out of the Aral Sea and the subsequent desertification of the area is an agony for all the peoples living in the sea basin.

The extent and difficult nature of the problems of water resources call for an integral and multisectoral approach and demand the promotion of co-operation between the states of the region and the international community.

The meeting of the Heads of States of Central Asia held in March 1993 in Kyzyl-Orda-city, where an agreement on joint actions to solve the Aral Sea crisis was signed, was an effort to solve these issues. The Interstate Council on Aral Sea Issues and its Executive Committee were set up, as well as the International Fund to save the Aral Sea. At the second meeting of the Heads of States of Central Asia, held in Nukus in January 1994, the 'program of specific actions to improve the environmental situation in the Aral Sea basin for the following three–five years considering social and political development of the region' was approved. At the third meeting, in Dashhauz in March 1994, the Interstate Council reported on the implementation of this program.

Being aware of the acuteness of the Aral problem and the need to adopt urgent measures for its rescue, the governments of the Central Asian republics, experts, scientists of the region and international institutions adopted on September 20, 1995, in Nukus-city the Declaration of the Central Asian States and International Organizations on the Sustainable Development of the Aral Sea Basin. It stipulates a strong commitment to the principles of sustainable development and focused its attention on the solution of such important problems as:

+ transition towards a more balanced and scientifically proved system of agriculture and forestry;
+ higher efficiency of irrigated agriculture through economically driven methods of water resource usage and the use of improved technologies in irrigation and environmental protection;
+ improvement of the system of integrated management of natural resources in the region.

The final goal is to design and implement a long-term strategy and program aimed at a solution to the Aral crisis based on the principles of sustainable development and the protection of the quality of life for people living in this area, providing in the long term a decent life for future generations.

Fourthly, air pollution is also a threat to ecological security in the Republic. According to expert investigations, approximately 4 million tons of hazardous substances are released into the atmosphere annually. Half of this is carbon monoxide, while hydrocarbon accounts for 15 per cent, sulphur dioxide 14 per cent, nitrogen oxide 9 per cent, solid substances 8 per cent and specific highly toxic harmful substances about 4 per cent. The growing concentration of carbon in the atmosphere leads to an increase in the average temperature of the air as a result of the global greenhouse effect.

For the Republic of Uzbekistan located in the arid zone the existence of such major natural sources of atmospheric dust as the Karakum and Kyzylkym deserts with frequent dust storms is typical. In recent decades due to the drying out of the Aral Sea another natural source of salt and dust displacement has emerged

A disastrous ecological situation exists in many districts of the Surkhandarya region of Uzbekistan as a result of the putting into operation, at the beginning of the eighties, in neighboring Tajikistan of an aluminum plant which releases large amounts of hydrogen fluoride, sulphurous gas, and nitric oxide into the atmosphere. The plant wastes located in the upper part along the valley on the Tajik-Uzbek border are spread by mountainous-valley winds far from its location, predominantly covering the territory of the districts adjacent to the border of the Republic: Saryasiya, Uzun, Denau, Altynsay of the Surkhandarya region.

Taking into account the significance of the ecological security threat for Uzbekistan and for the entire Central Asian region, the government pays great attention to the issues of environmental protection and the rational use of natural resources. Legal acts targeting the protection of the natural environment have been adopted. The national environmental protection measures of the Republic of Uzbekistan are complemented by extensive co-operation with other states and international organizations. A great number of international agreements regulating various aspects of environmental protection and the rational use of natural resources have been signed.

Uzbekistan is a fully fledged member of the CIS Intergovernmental Ecological Council created in accordance with the agreement signed by the Heads of States on February 8, 1992. Co-operation between the CIS countries within the framework of the above Ecological Council seeks the adoption of concerted and co-ordinated actions by member states in the domain of environmental protection.

Nowadays the Republic has expanded the state program on environmental protection and the rational use of natural resources in the run up to 2005. It serves as a basis for overall activity in the domain of the rational use of natural resources and environmental protection. The program identified ways to improve the ecological situation in the Republic and eliminate ecological tension in major cities and urban agglomerations.

Today the key ways to strengthen ecological safety are as follows:

1. Putting an end to air and water contamination by substances dangerous or adverse to human existence by designing and implementing adequate technology and by exercising strict control over all kinds of chemicals that are used in agriculture, forestry and other economic sectors and that deeply affect natural processes.

   The widespread implementation of water-saving irrigation techniques for agricultural crops, particularly cotton, will be of great importance. Discharges of collector-drainage waters should be regulated and the flow of waste to rivers and reservoirs should be stopped.

   It will be necessary to increase the responsibility of industrial enterprises for reducing soil, water and atmospheric pollution by dangerous substances; broadly using a special tax to put into operation modern efficient treatment facilities and to install ecologically efficient modern equipment for the complex utilization of raw materials up to finished product style.

2. The rational use of all types of natural resources securing the expansion of natural reproduction of renewable resources and the strictly calculated consumption of non-renewable ones.

   The rational use of mineral resources in the Republic is a

current problem, being one of the major factors of environmental protection. In the extraction and processing of mineral resources there are great losses, along with the incomplete utilization of primary raw materials. Securing the more rational and complete industrial development of mineral deposits through the replacement of old-fashioned equipment, the introduction of new technologies and reconstruction of individual facilities, workshops and production lines – all these issues are on the agenda. From the point of view of environmental protection, the progressive utilization of waste in the mining sector and the rehabilitation of damaged soil will also be of great significance.

3. The targeted and scientifically based modification of the natural environment over larger areas (regulation of river discharges and interbasin transfers of water, drying and water supply measures, etc.) in order to secure the efficient and integrated use of natural resources.

4. The preservation of natural genotype funds as a basis for growing new plants and improving animal breeding.

5. The creation of favorable conditions for people living in towns and other settlements by working out a system of scientifically based urban design and local planning, targeting the elimination of all negative implications of modern urbanization.

6. Drawing the attention of the international community to regional ecological problems due to the fact that ecological disasters do not recognize state borders, and that the Aral problem has genuinely become a problem of global scale, and its negative implications are now felt by the larger biological environment, destructively influencing the genotype funds over vast areas.

A task of paramount importance is to attract the resources and investment funds of international entities for our ecological enterprises.

The implementation of these and other effective environmental protection measures will permit the eradication in the foreseeable future of many deficiencies, flaws, and omissions in the domain of ecology inherited by the new state from the previous system, the elimination of the imminent threat of a global ecological crisis and the creation of the necessary conditions for an ecologically clean environment for the population of the Republic and the all-round development of a healthy young generation.

Part II
Conditions of stability and guarantees for progress

Chapter Eight

The revival of spiritual values and national self-awareness

No society can progress without developing and strengthening spiritual and moral values in the consciousness of its people.

Inherited cultural values have been a powerful source of spirituality for the peoples of the East for millennia. In spite of rigid ideological pressure over a long period, the people of Uzbekistan have managed to preserve their cultural values and their local traditions, which have been carefully transferred from generation to generation.

From the first days of our independence a major task, at state policy level, has been to revive the invaluable spiritual and cultural legacy that has been moulded by our ancestors over many centuries. We regard the revival of spiritual values, the return to the spiritual sources of the nation, to its roots, as a natural process in the growth of national self-awareness.

After gaining political independence and freedom, our people have become masters of their destiny, creators of their own history and holders of an original national culture. However, it is necessary to emphasize that the return to and restoration of spiritual and sacred values and traditions took place in difficult conditions – with the disintegration of the old imperial system and the building up of new social relations. After a period of more than a century of totalitarian dependence, this process initially took quite naturally the shape of the rejection of the recent past. But we were aware that a simple denial of the values of the former system introduced the danger of a political and cultural extremism leading to no creative program. At the same time, a thoughtless return to the values, traditions and tenor of the distant past can lead to another extreme: the denial of modern life, of the necessity to modernize society.

On the wave of this denial there was the further danger of a growth in an extremist opposition, which, in essence, could be an opposition to spirituality. Its political aspirations are a mixture of aggressive nationalism, religious intolerance and a pathological hatred of everything that is 'alien'. Our people perceived, through the extremist manifestations of those days, how aggressive that reaction was, and how great was the destructive force of the hatred of everything that did not fit in the narrow frames of perception of the separate militant politicized groups.

The danger of a return of such events dictated the need for a well-reasoned and balanced approach, the design and realization of a complex of complementary political, economic and cultural pro-grams, aimed at increasing the positive and creative nature of the spiritual revival. These programs were developed, first of all, with a different approach to the revived heritage, involving the nation's most important, positive and morally relevant traditions and customs, enriching universal values, and meeting democratization and modernization.

Thus, in the extreme situation of that period, particular impor-tance was given to the reduction or banning of emotional upheavals which could easily violate the fragile line behind which there could be inter-ethnic confrontations. This danger was visibly present in those days, and I am to this day convinced that only an appeal to the reason, will, tolerance and philanthropy of our people helped us to avoid an immense catastrophe.

Historical memory, the restoration of an objective and truthful history of the nation and its territory is given an extremely important place in the revival and growth of national self-consciousness and national pride. History can be a genuine tutor of the nation. The deeds and feats of great ancestors enliven historical memory, shape a new civil consciousness, and become a source of moral education and imitation. The history of Central Asia reveals many outstanding personalities who had political wisdom, moral valour, and a religious perception of the world.

Our great ancestors – Imam Bukhari, At-Termizi, Naqshband, Ahmad Yassavi, Al-Khorezmi, Beruni, Ibn Sina (Avicenna), Amir Timur (Tamerlane), Ulughbek, Babur (the first Mogul Emperor of India) and many others – have greatly contributed to the development of our national culture. They became the national pride of our people. But these men and their outstanding contribution to the development of world civilization are also known today in the whole world. Historical experience and traditions should become the values on which new generations are brought up. Our culture has become a center of attraction for the whole of mankind: Samarkand, Bukhara and Khiva are places of pilgrimage not only for scientists and connoisseurs of art, but for all people who are interested in history and cultural values.

Thanks to the efforts of Uzbek historians at the end of the 19th century and the beginning of the 20th, many important pages of our history, for instance, those of the Timurids' epoch, were opened anew. It is important to remember that the 'rehabilitation' of our past has actually already been carried out. The basic problem now is scientific objectivity and unprejudiced historical analysis.

It is especially necessary to mention the celebrations of the Amir Timur anniversary. How many times in the past when we read and heard about 'Timur – a conqueror', and 'Timur – a destroyer' did we ask ourselves: 'How could such a culture and economy flourish on our ground during his reign?' Only after gaining independence could we render proper veneration to and appraisal of our great ancestor. In this we have been supported by both our Central Asian neighbors and the international cultural community, for Timur's personality is a heritage not only for us, his descendants, but also for all peoples in our region, and for the whole of civilized mankind.

The ethnic, cultural and religious tolerance of our nation is another deep source of spiritual revival. For many millennia Central Asia has been a meeting-place where different religions, cultures and styles of living have coexisted. Ethnic tolerance and openness became natural patterns that were necessary for survival and for development. Even those who conquered this territory not only admired the culture of its nations, but also carefully adopted the traditions and elements of the state system that existed in the territory. It is precisely on this land that reciprocal enrichment of world cultures has occurred for many centuries. For centuries nomadic tribes coexisted with settled nations here, Iranic tribes with Turkic tribes, Muslims with Jews and Christians. Over the last two centuries, when even states that considered themselves to be 'civilized' and 'enlightened' stained themselves with massive massacres and religious persecutions, the land of Uzbekistan not only remained a place of peaceful unity for peoples and cultures, but it also gave shelter to persecuted peoples.

The present-day reforming and renovation of our social life has revealed rich layers of spiritual culture that have sharply shifted people's psychology towards national pride, and openness towards the world. This is a striking feature of the spirit of the people, which is fearless of integration but, on the contrary, seeks to be an organic but independent part of the world community.

The laying of the foundations of a 'common home' for all Uzbek peoples and the emergence of a new poly-ethnic community have been the most important results of five years of independence. The universal character of Uzbek culture and the revival of moral values and national self-consciousness have become the core of this community. The rebirth of the spirit of the Uzbek nation and the consolidation of the nation's moral ideals constitute a phenomenon showing a deep interrelation of national and universal features. Peoples who inhabit Uzbekistan have discovered a common philosophy without losing their originality. Hence there is a common moral core that has been the source of inter-ethnic harmony during the years of independence.

Although being historically and linguistically a part of the family of Turkic nations, our people have resolutely rejected the promises of pan-Turkism, along with the chauvinistic idea of a 'Great Turan'. For us Turan is a symbol of the cultural, but not the super-political unity of the Turkic-speaking nations of the region. Besides, we also have common cultural, historical and anthropological roots with the Tajik people, and this suggests that our culture is a unique synthesis of Turkic and Persian elements. Possessing such a legacy, together with the combination of high educational standards, urbanization and industrialization, and a traditional way of living, Uzbekistan has the potential to become the initiator of the cultural integration of the Central Asian states. Uzbekistan can also stand as a symbol of the spiritual links of many civilizations, and thus as a mediator in the West–East dialogue.

The revival of the spiritual-religious foundation of our society, the Islamic culture that contains the centuries-old experience of the moral consolidation of our people, is an important step on the path to self-identification and the restitution of historical memory and cultural-historical integrity. Old mosques are being reconstructed and new ones are built; educational centres are being expanded; religious literature is being published. However, the process of the revival of the national traditions of Islam and culture has been a vindication of the decision not to 'import' Islam from outside, not to politicize Islam and not to Islamize our politics. The Muslim culture of our region Transoxiana showed a spirit of ethnic tolerance and openness. Its ideal, described in the works of Farabi and Ibn Sina, was the Ideal City – a community of people united not only by religion, but also by culture and morals. The upholding of freedom of belief in our constitution not only dispelled fears of the possible overall 'Islamization' of Uzbekistan, but also contributed to the revival and normal development of other religions. An understanding of the spiritual originality of Islam in Central Asia requires a profound study of the pre-Islamic culture that is a part of our cultural wealth.

Spiritual revival should also embrace the attitude of the people to the land and its richness. In the areas where agriculture has for centuries been based on irrigation, the careful treatment of land and water is no less important a moral imperative than a careful attitude towards objects of civilisation. Soil, air, water, fire and the sun have traditionally been worshipped in Central Asia; they were accorded respect by all the religions of our ancestors, from Zoroastrianism to Islam. Unfortunately it is the ecological system of the region that has suffered the most damage over the last century. The traditional ethics of our forefathers regarding the utilization of nature (for example the banning of the defiling and wasting of water and land resources) were ignored.

The need to study and disseminate the reasonable and harmonious utilization of nature in the pre-Islamic cultures of the Central Asian peoples should be specially stressed. It is not accidental that our land was the birthplace of Zoroastrianism, which taught people to take care of the purity of rivers and the fertility of the soil. Other doctrines like Buddhism and Manichaeism also stressed the careful treatment of nature as one of the most important ways to the good society. So it is not surprising that we see similar ideas of harmony in the relationship between man and nature in the doctrines of Central Asian Sufism, which made such a contribution to the Muslim renaissance in Transoxonia.

The Dutch were able to reclaim fertile land from the sea, as they implemented their national model of a reasonable and creative attitude towards nature. This example has deep importance and implications for us, though in the case of the ecological disaster of the Aral Sea we will have to reclaim sea from land, not land from sea.

Another powerful source of spiritual values is the traditional ethics of family and the ties of relationship, the basic principles of which are respect for the old, mutual assistance and care for children. Regretfully these values were also seriously eroded during the Soviet period. Having banned private entrepreneurship and suppressed the transfer of professional skills in their fight against the power and influence of families, Soviet rule made it possible for families and clans to lose their traditional professional and economic 'niches'. As a result, these skills, and the moral norms that underpinned them, once blocked began to turn into socially ugly forms of clanship and nepotism. Assistance of relatives turned into an over-dependence and protectionism that impeded the development of society. The rebirth of family values and ties of relationship should not imply the perpetuation of obsolete family-generic relations, but the possibility of the economic, cultural and professional advancement of every family member.

The revival of spiritual values must also involve their adaptation to some of the values of the modern world and its 'global information' civilization. The positive values that modern civilization manifests are the values connected to the processes of building up a law-governed democratic society. Among them are the observance of fundamental human rights, like freedom of entrepreneurship, freedom of speech and freedom of the mass media. In considering the significance of these democratic values for our society, it should be stressed that they do not go against the grain of our nation either historically or ethno-culturally. On the contrary, such notions as entrepreneurship, free trade, social justice, mutual tolerance and respect for other people's opinions have deep historical roots in our land.

At the same time we stand against mechanical and blind copying. History suggests that this step is very dangerous for a nation's 'unprepared consciousness'. It is possible to *obtain* political freedom quickly and without any confrontation; this is proved by the acquisition of political sovereignty by the former Soviet Republics. It is also possible to *achieve* economic freedom quickly, and this we see in the industrially developed countries of East Asia. But to *secure* political freedom *within* a state is a process that requires a thoughtful, thorough and balanced approach, involving a lasting adaptation to the people's consciousness.

The most important aspect of modern democratic society with which the traditional values of our nation should be harmonized is social and market competition. In the process of promoting market structures, such competition may acquire repugnant forms and become a social danger. The shaping of this competition into civilized forms and competitive-creative capacities is possible through non-economic mechanisms, primarily cultural mechanisms. These should involve a synthesis of reviving national values and the assimilated desirable norms of modern civilization.

The recognition of an independent Uzbekistan by the world community, the broadening of the external political and economic activities of our state, and the comprehension that we are a fully-fledged nation within the family of nations, has become an additional reason for the rebirth of spiritual values and the potential of the Uzbek nation. Wide international contacts have not only created favorable ground for a deeper study of world culture and the assimilation of universal values, but they have also promoted the talent of the Uzbek nation in various fields and enabled it to reveal to the full some exceptional qualities, including enterprise and communication skills. Thanks to such contacts a new impulse has been given to the display and development of our traditional national hospitality.

The expansion of these links has allowed the Uzbeks to appreciate genuine spiritual and cultural values, both local and universal. Already now dissatisfaction is being felt throughout the population with the *ersatz* of some of Western 'art products' for 'cultural consumption' that have engulfed our viewers and readers since the end of the eighties. Such products have lost their attraction as 'forbidden fruit', which they had previously represented. The need for a better, more selective approach towards modern cultural values from abroad is growing.

The education of the population in the process of the assimilation of 'world democratic values' is of primary importance. *History convincingly demonstrates that only an educated, enlightened society is capable of appreciating all the advantages of democratic development, while poorly educated, ignorant people prefer an authoritarian, totalitarian system.* We must learn to treat delicately those cultural sources that provide possibilities for all social layers to assimilate the best examples of both national and international modern culture. The considerable success of Uzbekistan in the areas of music, and the pictorial, monumental and applied arts, which enjoy high recognition abroad, is significant. The wide dissemination and popularization of the best of both traditional and world culture should serve as a basis for the spiritual and moral education of the younger generation.

Independence has expanded the horizons of our population. Confronting the realities of history and modern life has obliged the Uzbeks to discard abstract and doctrinal stereotypes of moral principles, and to develop skills for the independent analysis and assessment of models of morality. 'Spiritual revival' is seen in the emergence of a new generation among the creative intelligentsia, whose way of thinking is determined by a spirit of independence. The questioning of old petrified dogmas does not imply a rejection of the past. It is the questioning of a one-sided and narrow way of thinking. If the nation is to develop it is compelled to address global problems of cultural construction and reconstruction, to be keenly interested in other peoples' fates and in their interrelationship, but yet to take into account national interests.

The future of our nation above all depends on the nation itself: on its spiritual energy and on the creative forces of its national consciousness. The natural aspiration for material well-being must not obliterate the need for spiritual and intellectual growth within the nation. But spirituality and enlightenment have always been strong forces among our people throughout its centuries-old history. The combination of these traditional spiritual-moral values with those of modern democratic society constitutes our guarantee for our future prosperity and for our successful integration within the world community.

Chapter Nine

Building up a state system and strengthening a defensive capability

The years of independence since 1991 have been a period of careful and intensive work in laying the foundations of a national state system for newly independent Uzbekistan. The long history of our state building was interrupted as a result of forced incorporation into the Russian Empire between 1865 and 1876. Only after obtaining independence has sovereign Uzbekistan become an equal entity in the world system and proceeded to promote a new statehood. Independence has enabled our people feel free in their Motherland, to recuperate genuine national values, and to set up their own national state system.

After obtaining independence our people faced acute problems needing to be resolved in order to create a new statehood based on the principles of democracy and the separation of powers, to consolidate a democratic law-governed state and a civil society. As its main priority Uzbekistan chose the values of democracy and personal freedoms, the provision of human rights, and the creation of a free market economy. It is impossible to reach the declared objectives without the total elimination of the remaining totalitarian ideological system and the rejection of old stereotypes. Therefore the tasks of paramount importance were:

1. The liquidation and dismantling of the old administrative command system.
2. The creation of the political, legal and constitutional foundations of a new state system and the consolidation of a new system of social relations and state bodies, both central and local.

This consolidation process took place in difficult conditions, both external and domestic. Touching domestic policy, we had to tackle a two-sided task: to build up a new state system and to implement large-scale political and economic reforms. The implementation of market reforms, as the experience of all the newly independent states shows, has heralded a decline in the economy and a reduction in living standards for a large part of the population, a reason for social tensions in our society. The non-constructive behavior of irresponsible and ambitious opposition forces with extremist attitudes, which have used democratic mottoes to provoke destabilization in our society, has made this problem particularly acute.

Among external political factors posing a threat to the construction of a new state were above all the military and political conflict in neighbouring Afghanistan and the painful processes of state formation in Tajikistan. Further escalation of these situations could affect the entire Central Asian region, particularly Uzbekistan.

The formation of the new state could not help being influenced by the social and political changes taking place in the newly independent states that have emerged in the post-Soviet territory, as well as by the relations between the CIS (Commonwealth of Independent States), and various attempts to impede our national sovereignty consolidation processes under the pretext of the acceleration and deepening of integration links. Apart from this, the consolidation of the new state system took place in conditions in which we were obliged to start, in many respects, from a zero level and to gain our place in the world community without sufficient experience of external political activity.

All these factors have created a difficult environment for the consolidation of the new independent state system of Uzbekistan. But today we may state with assurance that during these years the

96

foundations of the national state system have been laid down. The old administrative-command system and its corresponding bodies have been dismantled. Many of the bodies of political and economic management and regulation, which were the supporting elements of the old administrative-command system of the centralized planning and distribution economy, and were the principal barriers on the path to the consolidation of a new state system oriented to democratic values and principles and the creation of a free market economy, have been liquidated.

The adoption of the Constitution of the Republic of Uzbekistan in December 1992 was an event of paramount political importance in the life of our country, and a major step forward in the process of the consolidation of the new Uzbekistan. No state will become truly sovereign unless the principles of statehood, citizens' rights and freedoms, and the economic basis of social development are upheld in its basic law. The Constitution became the regulative basis and main pillar of our sovereign state.

A system of state bodies, which radically differ from those of the former totalitarian system, has been created, based on the principle of separation of powers: the legislative, executive and judicial. A legal basis of truly democratic norms and procedures has been set up, aimed at preventing a return to authoritarianism and totalitarianism. The new system of executive bodies differs radically from the previous system: they are deprived of planning and distribution functions, and play the role of the co-ordinator and regulator of economic policy. Numerous ministries have been replaced by more flexible and market-oriented economic amalgamations, associations, corporations and holding companies.

A new system of local government has been created that has at its core *khokims*, which combine the functions of executive power and representative power. An orderly system of local authorities is unconceivable without self-governing agencies, the core of which constitute citizens' gatherings – the *mahallas*. These agencies were created with regard to the historical traditions and 'mentality' of the people, for whom the significance of a *mahalla* as an important social self-governing agency has always been great. The *mahalla* plays an important role in the promotion of neighbourliness, and respect in relations between people. It protects the social interests of citizens, providing concrete assistance to the most needy groups of the population. At the same time current conditions require that the functions of the *mahalla* be renewed. The fact is that *mahallas* should provide effective support for the implementation of economic and democratic transformations.

In accordance with the Constitution, for the first time in Uzbekistan's history free elections, on a plurality basis, to the Parliament of the Republic – Oli Majlis – and to local representative bodies were held in accordance with the new democratic electoral system. The result was the creation (and effective performance) of the legislative branch of state power represented by the Oli Majlis and the local councils of people's deputies.

As the result of legal reforms, using the basic law, the judicial system of the Republic has been set up as an independent and separated power branch. New structures of judicial power were created and the competence of the courts was expanded. Following the new state's strategic purposes and principles of democratic development, a system of law enforcement bodies and national security bodies has been practically created from scratch. The establishment of the Armed Forces of Uzbekistan was an important achievement in the consolidate processes of the national state system. Institutional structures regulating external relations, such as the Ministry of Foreign Affairs and the Ministry for External Economic Relations, the National Bank for External Economic Activity and a network of other specialized institutions, have been set up.

For the first time in the history of Uzbekistan the post of President of the Republic was introduced. The presidency became the core element in the political system of new Uzbekistan and took the central place in the system of state authority bodies. Presidential authority, which unites the powers of the President as Head of State and Head of the Executive, has become a key element in the development of the new Uzbek state, a warrant for stability in society and the successful advance of Uzbekistan along the path of reforms.

The adoption of the Constitution and the energetic legislative activity of recent years has established a solid basis for the formation of a law-governed state that guarantees the equality of all citizens before the law, and the supremacy of the law. It is noteworthy that the very essence of the state has radically changed. The state has become the main initiator and co-ordinator of the reforms, the principal conductor of new ideas in the life of society and the most active participant in society's renovation.

Today, the reform of the democratic state system is conditioned, above all, by the fact that further democratization of social life is the most important current priority, involving the diversification and strengthening of political institutions and non-governmental organizations. In the new environment, the primary task of the state authorities is to seek new forms of co-operation with political parties, non-governmental and social organizations, and other emerging institutions of a civil society. We seek new and effective ways to transfer some of the power from the center to local government, maintaining at the same time the efficient performance of the central state bodies. Local government in its turn must identify the possibilities for enhancing its role by transferring to it part of central government's powers and functions.

The initial stages of reform saw the concentration of basic power in the hands of the state (primarily the executive power). The current stage of democratic transformation involves a long-term strategy of political, economic and social development that will see radical changes in the state's role, in the interest of the ultimate objective of our democratic development – a civil society. We are creating a system in which a strong central state authority can concentrate its efforts on basic issues of national concern such as defence, the security of the state and of its citizens, external policy, and the shaping of legal, financial, currency and taxation systems, while responsibility for decisions on other problems and issues is gradually transferred from the center to the regions, from state-authority bodies to social organizations and citizens' self-governing bodies.

At the same time, in present conditions, the further strengthening of Uzbekistan's new state system through clearer identification of the role of the state in the system of political institutions in society is of particular importance, especially from the point of view of consolidating the bases of national security, preserving stability and maintaining the steady political and economic development of the country.

National security, which is understood as (a) the guaranteed protection of interests of vital importance to the Republic of Uzbekistan and of the rights and freedoms of its citizens against external and internal threats, and (b) a comprehensive set of measures that have as its components a strong state, citizens' self-governing bodies, and a wide network of non-governmental structures. The interior threat to national security is most effectively solved through the strengthening of democratic non-governmental and civil structures designed to channel the efforts of an active citizenry in order to remove the danger of illegal political extremism. However, the acknowledgement that the state bears primary responsibility for the provision of national security makes it necessary to concentrate on the reform of state bodies to avoid a situation where decentralization processes lead to regional separatism, and the processes of social democratization serve as a basis for upheavals of political extremism under different slogans.

External forces cause the greatest threat to the national security, sovereignty and territorial integrity of the country today. Potential sources of military danger are armed conflicts on the southern borders of our country. This places our defensive capability among the most important conditions that will provide national security and stability: not only for Uzbekistan, but for the whole region as well.

The defensive potential of a state consists of the combination of its political, economic, military, scientific and moral potential. The foundations of our policy in this field have been fixed in the military doctrine approved by the Oli Majlis following its broad discussion by all layers of our society. Our people endorsed its defensive character and its basic principles. It consists of the unwillingness to use aggressive force or threaten to use it; the provision of a defensive capability of a level of reasonable sufficiency; undertakings to observe the principles and standards of international law and to comply with undertakings under international agreements.

A major element of a state's defensive capability is its armed forces – their combat power and degree of readiness to prevent aggressors from unleashing military conflicts and to overcome the aggressors if the country is attacked. The objective should be the gradual creation of a professional army and air force with adequately trained fighters, loyal to their nation, and capable of defending the honor of the Motherland to the end. We need armed forces small in number, but mobile and well-equipped with modern weapons, with a balanced fighting potential, able to offer an adequate response on the ground and in air space to a possible aggressor, given the geostrategic situation of our country and the geographical particularities of its territory.

The power and capacity of a country's armed forces are composed of four factors.

1. The first factor is the quantity and quality of the personnel – the latter of which is determined by the extent of their professionalism, moral and psychological health, physical condition and discipline. The composition and extent of our armed forces should correspond on the one hand to the existing military and political situation in the region and to possible threats from outside, and on the other hand to the resources of our state.

Professional training and an adequate teaching base are essential in ensuring the quality of the forces. We need a military training system that produces physically and morally strong members of our society, patriots of their Motherland, who have mastered both the achievements of world civilization and the spiritual values of our nation. Much has been done in this field. A system for training officers' cadres for various armed services has been created. We have four military colleges, including one for training pilots, and one for training specialists in communication systems. The Armed Forces Academy, established in 1994, trains officers at a high level of military education. This system is based on the latest achievements of military art and experience in military action, worldwide. However, the peculiarities of the Central Asian region should be taken into careful consideration; it is necessary to learn from and assimilate the military arts of our great ancestors: Jalaluddin Manghuberdi, Timur Malik, Amir Timur, Babur and others.

2. The second factor is the quantity and quality of armaments. The state has undertaken measures to provide the armed forces with

sophisticated weaponry, and to maintain their quality at a high level, to ensure superiority over potential enemies.

3. The third factor is the military infrastructure. Systems of management; communications, combat, rear and technical provision; and the basing of our troops of different branches have been set up. Our operational equipment is being improved. Today it is adequate to the current structure, number and location of troops.

4. Fourthly, of great significance for the defensive capability of any country is the creation of conditions for the rapid restructuring of industry to meet the requirements of mobilization plans and mobilization resources to equip combat missions in case of large-scale aggression. Thus a strong economy and industry is the basis of a strong defensive capability.

The role of external economic and political factors in strengthening Uzbekistan's defensive capability and military security is also crucial. In modern conditions security may be exclusively collective, being provided by joint actions of states, by unifying their possibilities. That is why Uzbekistan is ready to take part in peacekeeping operations carried out under the aegis of the UN and OSCE. That is why Uzbekistan was one of the initiators of a collective security system in the region. One of the first treaties of this kind between CIS member-states was signed in Tashkent in May 1992.

However, Uzbekistan, being a member of the non-aligned nations' movement, does not participate in any military-political blocs, regards this stance as a guarantee of national security and peace and stability in the region, and opposes the creation of a military-political bloc on CIS territory. We bear in mind that such bloc formation might return the world to the 'cold war'.

We are determined to build up relations aimed at strengthening the national security of Uzbekistan and resisting external threat, on the principle of the preservation of general security and regional stability, on the agreed basis with those states whose vital interests are directly concerned. I would like to stress that the signing of similar military-political agreements should ensure the complete sovereignty, territorial integrity and inviolability of the existing borders of our country.

In July 1994 Uzbekistan joined NATO's program 'Partnership for Peace', which is aimed at creating a broad system of collective security and stability, including within the Central Asian region. Co-operation with NATO enables us to be aware of military-political events, to have access to investigations and research carried out within the framework of this alliance, and to take part in the activities of NATO countries (e.g. the joint training of military units). All this contributes not only to a higher level of combat preparedness of our military units and to the assimilation of advanced combat, which will raise the defensive capability of our country, but also to the strengthening of our state's links with economically developed democratic countries.

While promoting a wide network of bilateral and multilateral co-operation with foreign countries and international organizations, it is clear that Uzbekistan should also be more active in its military-political and military-technical co-operation with them.

An effective solution to the problems of defensive capability cannot be implemented within the patterns of a 'sole agency', but requires the involvement of the many organizations and institutions that are in charge of military infrastructure, the defence industry, external policy and the precise co-ordination of all these agencies with each other. It also requires the giving up of individual plans by every agency and program for the promotion of separate elements of a defensive capability, and the transition to building *a common comprehensive plan* to ensure military security and defensive capability. In conditions of limited resources and means, this makes it needful to use them efficiently to secure an acceptable level of defensive capability.

The Uzbekistan National Security Council plays an important role in the co-ordination of ministry and agency performance in the implementation of a common comprehensive plan for military security and defensive capability.

Owing to the variability of internal and external conditions, for instance demographic features, armaments and our technical level, the defensive capability of our country, the prospects for its development, and the experience and practice in this sphere of other states demand continual attention and systematic assessment.

Understanding and realizing all these principal provisions concerning the building of our state system and defensive capability under definite conditions, along with a continued awareness of all the players on this field, are the necessary pre-conditions for ensuring the stable and sustainable development of Uzbekistan.

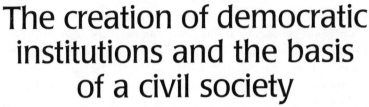

Chapter Ten

The creation of democratic institutions and the basis of a civil society

The last decade of the 20th century will be entered in the history of mankind as an epoch of great transformations.

1. Colonialism, apartheid and the system of socialism with its claims for the world expansion of the communist ideology are slipping away into the past.
2. Many newly independent states, whose voices are becoming louder among countries of the world community, have been emerging.
3. The traditional balance of world power is being corrected on account of the growing role and significance of the countries of the Asian continent, which are contributing their vision to the problems, standards and values of world development.
4. The principles of democratic development are becoming more universal, and their need and effectiveness cannot be disputed. In addition, different individual models of advancement to democracy are beginning to play an ever-growing role on the world's stage.

Such tremendous changes in our ever more complicated and multipolar world directly and indirectly determine the socio-political and economic development of the Republic of Uzbekistan. The general policy of an ever-growing openness and commitment to democratic principles and universal values and norms not only leaves its mark on the processes of democratization of social life in the Republic, but also influences the perception of these changes by the world community, thus shaping a new image of the modern Republic of Uzbekistan. The international community is increasingly aware of the significance and the growing role of Uzbekistan, and of its balanced and consistent internal and external policy on stabilizing the situation and preventing an escalation of tensions in the controversial Central Asian region.

Democratic principles and institutions are dominating more and more in all spheres of our life, and acquiring their specific contents under the specific conditions of Uzbekistan and the region. The creation of democratic institutions in the social and political sphere of society is directed at reforming the political system, at making the reforms irreversible, and at supporting the democratization processes of ordinary social life.

The Constitution of the Republic of Uzbekistan serves as a legal guarantee for the democracy-oriented development of the country. It expresses and supports, in a concentrated form, the relationships and interests existing in society. The importance of the basic law to the consolidation of democratic society is because it is essentially oriented to the needs, interests, rights and freedoms of the individual, not to an abstract 'society' or 'nation'. The Constitution presupposes the individual as the superior value, and thus politically provides a reasonable legal expression of the relationship between citizen, society and state, and thereby of stability in the country and of the creation of a civil society.

For us a civil society is a social space where the law commands but does not oppress, and contributes to the self-development of a person, to the realization of his interests, to the maximum implementation of his rights and freedoms. But the infringement of other people's rights and freedoms is outlawed. Thus legal freedom and legal obedience act together, complementing each other. The laws of the state must not harm the rights of a citizen, but the laws must be observed by all unconditionally.

The democratic content of power structures is determined, to a large extent, by how the problem of citizens' participation in state management is solved. The legislative basis for the realization of this participation in Uzbekistan has been set up. But it is still necessary to promote a climate in which citizens understand and use the right to participate in state management. Only then will state officials properly feel their responsibility towards society and its citizens. For this reason, it is necessary to encourage the political activeness of citizens. In a stable and sustainable system all the legal democratic conditions for the realization of citizens' political interests are created, and a large part of the population is taking part in the political life of the country on a voluntary or a professional basis. This democratic process of citizens' participation in the political life of Uzbekistan is gaining strength.

Under the conditions of the transitional period, when the process of the formation of the basis of a civil society is under way, the creation of such democratic institutions as a multi-party system and other social organizations formed to interpret the interests of different layers of Uzbekistan's population acquires a primary significance. In this context the role of the state is to eliminate all obstacles that impede the growth of those political parties and social movements without which it is difficult to imagine the establishment of representative democracy in the Republic.

However, it is necessary to remember that the *quality* of democracy is not determined by the growing number of parties. It is important to create an agreed political space for those political parties that will truly express and defend the interests of many social layers. *Through the concentration and accumulation of social interests the formation of parties, their number and their specific programs and goals should occur naturally. The basic and the sole principle for the existence of any political party should be respect of and observance of the Constitutional norms of the state.*

It is of paramount importance that political parties and social movements shall as soon as possible achieve the functions of democratic institutions serving as the main links between the people and the state. This will come about when the citizens' involvement in the social, political, economic and cultural problems of society is evident: their civilized participation in this or that party or movement.

Concerning the need to maintain stability in society, it is impossible to avoid the issue of opposition as a political institution, the existence of which is a normal manifestation in any democratic society. However, it is important that it should have a proper organizational design, have an adequate legal status, have respect for constitutional and legislative norms, be constructive and responsible in its actions and plans for a stable and sustainable political and social regime, and have clear alternative projects of state design. Thus, it would hardly be possible to describe as constructive the opposition of ambitious people who consider themselves offended not to be given cherished positions within the government, and who in pursuing clan and local interests oppose everybody and everything that happens in the country. Instead of there being a constructive and civilized counterbalance to the present government in the decision-making processes that society faces, there are attempts at illegal confrontation not only with official authorities but also with existing laws and the constitution of the state. Nevertheless I believe that the formation of a democratic opposition is a question of time, being in essence part of the painful process of the consolidation of the democratic institutions in Uzbekistan – as in other states undergoing the period of transition from a totalitarian system to a free society.

The social and political stability of a country greatly depends on public opinion, which is greatly influenced by another important social institution – the mass media. Today quite obviously we need to reform radically the activity of the mass media in Uzbekistan, because their performance does not meet present-day demands by reflecting the deep transformation and democratization of economic and political life in the country.

The process of converting the mass media into a real 'fourth power' is a controversial process everywhere. Stereotypes of the old mentality still exist, the overcoming of which will be accompanied by an exhausting struggle with ideology, psychology, and personal ambitions. In fact, the new social, political and economic environment in the country sets quite new, previously unknown tasks for the mass media. How then do we see the active role of the mass media in our society today?

Firstly, it is necessary to put in place everything necessary to allow the mass media to secure their proper place in the political, economic and cultural life of society, and to guarantee the social and legal protection of the journalists' activities. It is necessary to review the process of journalists' professional training, to help them to learn updated methods and procedures in obtaining, analyzing, processing and disseminating information to the public, in order to ensure that the mass media are capable of giving free and objective expression to diverse views on events in the country, of being impartial inter-mediaries between the authorities and society, and of being active and consistent champions of the interests of individuals and society.

Secondly, there is the need to upgrade both the legislative basis regulating the performance of mass media and the mechanisms facilitating their effective functioning. At the same time there is needed legislative protection of the mass media's interests and their individual representatives, ensuring their right to access to sources of information.

The establishment of non-state-owned periodicals and TV channels, and also international assistance in the professional training of the most talented journalists, will be of great importance in ensuring the freedom of the press and the other mass media.

The key element in the overall democratization of society, and in economic life in particular, has been the transformation of proprietorship relations (mostly those relating to private property), regarded as the most fundamental social relation. It is precisely through new proprietorship relations that political, eco-nomic and social renovation mostly reveals itself. When we emphasize the priority of democratization and the promotion of social institutions in the economic sphere, we proceed predomi-nantly from the fact that it is possible to maintain social and political stability in the country only if economic stability is provided. Nevertheless, it is impossible to continue the process of economic reform and the renovation of society without truly promoting of social democracy.

The stage-by-stage reformation of society creates opportunities to secure consistency between the different entities of the political system. The state functions as chief reformist and assists in every possible way to raise the potential of the emerging democratic institutions and elements of civil society, identifying and imple-menting social interests gradually and harmoniously, and seeking the optimal functioning of social, political and economic links.

The processes of building up democratic institutions and the creation of key elements of civil society are impossible without studying and implementing universal democratic principles. The assimilation of the democratic values that mankind has been working out over millennia is a major condition for true reform in society. If the general concept of democracy implies the power of the majority in the interests of all, and respect for minorities, a more detailed analysis shows that democracy is also individuals' visions of their own freedom and independence, the protection of the interests and rights of every individual against arbitrary restrictions and actions, and the form of citizens' self-governing.

Beyond definitions of democracy is the problem of to what extent it is capable of surviving. The ideal is that it should permeate every moment of our lives and become a basic component of our existence. However, we believe that by giving a 'green light' to *all* the principles of democracy – free elections, freedom of association, expression, assemblies etc. – on unprepared legal, economic, social and political soil, we would risk the stunting of real democracy.

There are at least three effective criteria for defining the degree of democracy in a society: the extent to which the public is informed about decision-making processes, the extent to which governmental decisions are under the control of the public, and the extent to which ordinary citizens take part in state management. If there is no progress in these three fields, then all discourse about democracy is either mere populism or simply a political game. But this progress does not happen overnight.

Rights such as those to take part in the management of state affairs and to have freedom of assembly and association will remain notional without an adequate economic, political and, predominantly, legal space. Democracy is impossible without a strictly adjusted system of laws. At the same time, the adoption of laws and the performance of the government and all its officials should, without exception, be examined through the prism of the above democratic criteria. This is very important because democracy is the key element of a law-governed state. A law-governed state does not imply simply a formal legality, but is a comprehensively functioning system based on the recognition of the person as the superior value.

In order to ensure the comprehensive functioning of the political system and its further liberalization, it is necessary to achieve a sound functioning of all its structural components: its individuals, its political institutions, its social groups and its population layers. That is why the methods, mechanisms and rates of the liberalization of the political system acquire an extraordinary importance, given the necessity to sustain this process. Every section, every level of the political system requires a specific approach when designing the development and liberalization strategy. Haste and the absence of a systematic approach will turn out to have dangerous and unpredictable consequences.

The transition from one social system to another is necessarily accompanied by an intense level of new political activity. This is quite natural. The new society will manifest all at once all accumulated social contradictions. Precisely in this period it is most important how, by whom and where the flow of political activity, political interests and the emotion of the population are to be directed. It is common knowledge that it is easier to destroy than to build. The famous motto 'Raze everything to the ground, and after that . . .' was adopted by many 'democratic' leaders. But unfortunately many of them implemented only the first part of this famous recipe. Uzbekistan has selected another route to democracy. In identifying the basic tasks and goals in building up an independent law-governed state, we have repeatedly emphasized that the key to achieving the bright heights of civilization and progress is a free and harmoniously developed person who has assimilated the best of our cultural and historical heritage, our humane traditions and our commitment to democratic values and standards.

Already in that period of general social euphoria and revolutionary demolition there grew the strong conviction that the destruction of structures without careful analysis was fraught with dangerous consequences for the destiny of an independent state system. *Our goal — as we underlined at the outset of the nineties — was not to lose that which has been created with the labour of many generations, to keep all that is best, to rearrange that which does not meet our national interests and our independence and to enrich the existing structures with new contents. The rich culture of the Uzbek nation, its educational system and its scientific establishment could not*

111

be dismissed merely as the totalitarian heritage. The course we have chosen is to re-orient these systems towards a new ideological platform based both on the centuries-old traditions, customs, culture and language of the Uzbek people, and on the achievements of world civilization. The spirituality we promote – we underline it once again – ought to nurture in people's hearts and minds faith in the future, love of the Motherland, humanism, courage, tolerance and fairness.

This approach may seem to be 'traditionalistic'. But is 'traditionalism' a bad thing? In fact, the traditional Oriental culture, which our people have been nurturing for thousands of years and which we seek to retain, differs a great deal from its Western counterpart. The main thing is to what extent traditional culture is open to and capable of assimilating other values. Viable cultures are not only authentic and integral, but are also capable of mutual enrichment.

Any confusion between a traditional culture and a 'patriarchal' culture should be dismissed. A traditional culture combines two opposite but mutually complementary trends: a certain closeness, resistant to ephemeral external fashions, and, at the same time, a certain openness, implying great possibilities for future development. Extensive, taught knowledge of the particularities of the development of Uzbek culture and of world cultures should serve as the foundation for the cultural and spiritual revival of our young state.

It should be stressed that democracy is not merely a theory or a political process. It should more importantly be a nation's way of living, its 'mentality', traditions, psychology. Democracy may be 'declared', may be 'imposed' from top to down, but in this way it will not become part of our real life. Democracy should become the *value* of society, and the value of *every person* in society. This will not be a quick process. Democracy that has not found its place within the culture of a nation will not become a component of its way of living. A long-lasting spade-work process to learn the principles of democracy is necessary. Many states have needed many generations replacing each other to reach this level.

Luckily, Uzbekistan has a tradition of such democratic development. Therefore, the stage-by-stage transition to democracy will not only give stability, but also naturally promote the careful retention and cultivation of the emerging shoots of a civil society. There is a profound understanding that the traditional culture and character-istics of our people, its psychology and social organization will be the most favorable factors for democratic consolidation.

There is one more point to make. Even in countries where there is a stable democracy some negative consequences of individualism are acutely felt. We in Uzbekistan must not underestimate the significance of this. Individualism penetrates everybody's psychol-ogy, acts selectively and definitely and uses all the mechanisms of the conscious and the unconscious of an individual. It is not surprising that there is a growing inclination on the part of some young people to search for ways of living involving trading in bazaars, bringing into town goods in order to sell them and using other forms of primitive market relations, instead of seeking learning and obtaining high professional skills. Manifestations of nihilism and egoism bordering on cruelty are not accidental. This, in our view, reveals the shortcomings of these individuals' education and their surround-ing environment. What measures can and should be taken against this, alongside legal exertion?

In the sphere of ideology, there cannot be a vacuum. Our ideology of national independence, worked out on the basis of the most progressive political and cultural traditions, both local and international, is able to oppose the pernicious influence of indivi-dualism. Ideological work, propaganda of the ideas of independence, high spirituality, morality and culture should be a complex, practical effort. Morality and spirituality should not be treated as abstract categories, as the work and province of a lot of writers and educators. The shaping of a citizen with high morals is a cause for all of us.

We have every ground to be confident that the high objectives related to building up a democratic state based on a free market economy in close interrelation with formation of an open civil society and civil self-government is a feasible task. The ground for this is our rich history; our great culture that has contributed enormously to world civilization; our natural and intellectual potential; the high spiritual and moral values of our people; their

113

diligence, openmindedness and desire to occupy their deserved place within the world community.

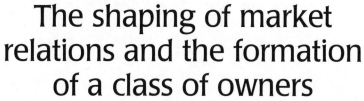

Chapter Eleven

The shaping of market relations and the formation of a class of owners

Economic changes based on a decisive departure from the command-administrative distribution system and a move to a free market economy are some of the principal new approaches to the reform of society. Our own model of transition to market relations takes into account the specific reality and the specific peculiarities of Uzbekistan, its traditions and customs, and aims at eradicating the evils of the past: its one-sided, hypertrophied economic development. At the same time, our model aims to absorb all the positive features that have been accumulated by those countries which have traveled the difficult road of renovation and change.

An analysis of the past period of our independent development reveals the solid basis of the Uzbek model of reforms. Today this is acknowledged by authoritative international economic organizations. But most importantly, everyday experience also proves its appropriateness. Post-Soviet reality obliges many post-Soviet leaders, politicians and economists to refer to the principles and features of our model of market reforms. What are the main issues that emerge?

First of all, the over-politicization of the economy, by submitting it to ideology and to the interests of various parties and movements, hampers the development of economic reforms and changes in the market.

115

Secondly, it is difficult to provide a smooth transition from any administrative-command system to the principles of a market economy when the regulating role of the state is ignored. However, it goes without saying that when market structures become stronger through the provision of irreversible reforms, the influence of state structures will standardize and decrease appropriately.

Thirdly, every day proves the necessity (especially if we take into account past Soviet experience) of changing people's mentality, to strengthen the values of democracy and to achieve obedience to the rule of law. This becomes important when we take into account the growing corruption of society, and the growth of efficiently organized criminal systems in all of these countries.

Fourthly, experience itself proves that in those places where the importance of strong social policy as a constituent element of market reforms is underestimated, social tension and confrontation springs up and this, in turn, results in a discrediting of the concept of reform.

Fifthly, popular wisdom says: 'You can't limit limitless areas' – there is no need to try to solve all problems. But a stage-by-stage progress is important in solving problems, taking into account their priority and significance. This, on the one hand, makes it possible to use limited resources effectively and purposefully, without scattering them. On the other hand, it makes it possible to evaluate and see in proper perspective the results of one's activity and to introduce proper corrections, when it is necessary, to the reform program.

I shall cite some illustrations from the life of our Republic. It was difficult to solve the 'macro' problems, quite apart from solving the problems of providing the country with oil products, gas, fuel and grain. While solving the global strategic task of converting the economy to 'market rails', we did everything possible to avoid a sharp decrease in production. The suppression of inflation, the restriction of monetary mass and of the deficit of the state budget – all these are mandatory and important requirements for the proper functioning of the market mechanism, of economic, financial stabilization and reliable growth.

The time-rates and methods of achieving these goals are vitally important for us. If these goals are achieved at the expense of a catastrophic decrease, stagnation and degradation of production and, as its consequence, an unmanageable growth of the state debt, a systematic and growing non-execution of the budget, and the impoverishment of the majority of the population, then it will be understood that we do not consider this as an acceptable and stable situation.

When in most of these states the problem non-payment of salaries, pensions and allowances is today turning into the threat of social explosion, then the causes must be looked for in miscalculations and mistakes that were made in the implementation of the selected course of reforms: blind, thoughtless copying of useless schemes and models of market transformations.

It is appropriate to dwell on one more important question for us. This is about state support for domestic goods producers in the setting up of a market economy. It is well known that, at the beginning of the reforms, many countries in the post-Soviet area directed most of their internal and loaned currency resources first of all to expand the importing of consumer goods. This resulted in the departure, voluntarily or not, of domestic producers from the internal market. The result was that enormous currency assets were simply spent on food: as a result of its decrease and sometimes of the collapse of our national agriculture.

We have chosen the most difficult road. In the first stages of the reforms we had to restrict somewhat the consumer market and at the same time direct assets and resources to the structural transformation of the economy. We created a modern, technologically equipped base both for export oriented production and for filling our domestic market with home-made goods. The main portion of state and loan assets is directed to investments and the delivery of new technology and equipment to the Republic. Already this policy is yielding its fruit: the automobile plant in Asaka; the Bukhara oil refinery; the exploitation of the Kokdumalak and Mingbulak reserves; the joint construction with foreign partners of dozens of textile and spinning factories; the production of alcohol in Andijan,

Kokand and Janghiyul; the sugar plant in the Khorezm region; the Kizilkum phosphoric group of enterprises; the Kungrad soda plant in the Karakalpak Republic; the reconstruction of the Uzbek group of enterprises of refractory and heat-resistant materials in the Almalyk and Navoi mining-metallurgical works; enterprises of the chemical industry; the construction of new roads and railroads; new tele-communications systems; the organization of public services and amenities in cities and villages; and also dozens of new enterprises in the country's food and local industries.

The first, most difficult years of hard, single-minded work to create a solid economic base for our country are all behind. Much has been done to open up Uzbekistan to the world, to create a legal and 'communication' base for co-operation with and integration into the world economy.

The experience of economic reform gained during the first period of our independence allows us to draw a number of important conclusions. These conclusions will serve as a basis for the future further democratization of reform.

1. The first conclusion is that it is necessary to comprehend a very simple truth. We cannot single-mindedly and dynamically advance along the road of renovation and progress without creating the proper conditions for advancing the interests of the individual. That is why providing the economic freedom of people and their enterprises is a priority for us.

It is possible to overcome the grave consequences of the totalitarian legacy, to overcome our economic crisis and to impart economic stability, only if a wide range of targeted economic reforms are implemented. But all our people must be widely involved in our reform processes. Reforms must be an essential part of the life of every free-marketeer, every employee, every progressively-thinking person in the Republic. We must positively give up the discredited administrative-command principles of management, the faulty centralized distributive system, the old 'levelling psychology' and, above all, the psychology of *dependency*.

The main heritage of the past must be eradicated: the distorted understanding of a human being's place in society; that he is a small

118

screw and that all his problems must be solved by a government. This understanding inevitably reduces the value of all his activities, and the manifold possibilities of his own labor. The detriment of this legacy is that it was accepted that if 'the state' was rich, then the family would be rich, and every person would be rich. It is difficult to believe that with this sort of attitude it will be possible to achieve effectiveness in individual production and labor. This outlook is still very firm in the minds of many people: our state is rich, it will feed us. Only the transition to market relations is today capable of liberating our people's creative and labor potential. We must overcome their *dependency* psychology, to recreate their lost sense of *ownership*.

2. The second conclusion is that the reforms will yield sensible results only when property issues are solved, and when a true middle class has emerged. When analyzing the issues of creating an economically stable society, it is necessary to bear in mind the role which business and the class of owners play in the reconstruction of state, and in ensuring social and political stability. It is the middle class that is the backbone of civil society.

At issue here are numerous forms of property. First of all, private property, which is the *economic* basis of sound democracy in any state. Then its *political* basis is the presence of a substantial middle class who own the means of production. We connect the whole process of economic reform with the initially important task of creating a real class of owners in the Republic. If a person does not feel he is a real owner, he will not fight as an owner to protect his rights or to maintain the standard of his own work, or to sustain stability in society.

3. The third conclusion is that the class of real owners emerges through the creation of a many-levelled economy: through the consecutive implementation of denationalization, privatization and the stimulation of the development of small and private business, and the creation of a securities market. The specific features of our area, the high level of labor redundancy, the developed agricultural and raw-materials base, as well as the traditions and mentality of our nation, all these encourage the progressive development of small and family businesses, and private entrepreneurship.

Small business means the appearance of a middle-class entrepreneurship which will help to normalize economic and political reality. It will provide the Republic's market with all necessary consumer goods and services. These are new jobs. Only by sponsoring the nation-wide development of small and private business can we solve one of our most acute problems, the provision of employment for the population, especially in the rural areas, which have redundant labor resources. We can create a wide net of small enterprises using the historical roots and mentality of the nation. These enterprises will not only provide the domestic market with consumer goods but will also produce competitive goods for external markets. Thus, essentially we must try to create a market where small and middle-size business, being the most mobile, flexible and easily transformed sphere of the economy, will take the leading role in the *production* structure of the country as well as in its *export* structure.

For the increase of the effectiveness and productivity of individual farms, the rendering of actual state help is important for the realization of this policy. We proceed from the point of view that small and middle enterprises must be created not on a primitive, outdated base but on a high-quality and advanced technical base. New sources for their development should be constantly found, both through attracting foreign investment and using domestic sources and bank credits.

During these last years of reform, the legal conditions and institutional structures have been created in Uzbekistan that should render assistance to small and middle business development. Among these are: the Chamber of Goods Producers and Entrepreneurs, Business Fund, Insurance Agency 'Madad', a net of consulting, engineering and leasing firms and companies, and business-incubators. Small and middle enterprises have already become a reality. By the beginning of 1997 the number of private and small enterprises was more than 100,000. Besides, more than 19,500 dehkans' (farmers) economies were established.

4. The fourth conclusion is that, according to the experience of countries with a developed market structure, the main mass of middle class ownership is formed by attracting citizens' free

monetary assets to the security markets, and to profitable bank deposits. By observing the state of the security markets we can assess how dynamically the process of market relations is performing. By participating in security markets, free monetary assets are involved in turnover and this promotes such significant aspects of economic stabilization as the strengthening of monetary circulation and, hence, of the national currency.

The main thing is that participation in fund markets promotes the population's interest in purchasing securities, and promotes the habits and the culture of dealing with them. It is important that people think of themselves as stockholders not only because they own shares, but because they are real proprietors of part of the nation's property and, as owners, have the right to affect the productive financial activity of their enterprises.

One more thing. The achievement of our goals in regard to the development of security markets in the Republic is possible only under conditions of an accelerated development of *secondary* security markets and under conditions of our entry into international fund and currency markets.

5. The fifth conclusion is that we are building a *law-governed* state. Thus, a reformed economy should be based on a strong legislative and regulative base. Only the existence of a strong legislative base for the reform process makes the reforms stable and non-reversible. We should never allow reforms to be based on a violation of rights, and on unsanctioned interests and actions. It is well known what results bureaucracy and command management bring when law and order are violated.

If it is necessary to adjust the course of reform, if there is something to correct or change, then we should first change the regulations and make the necessary amendments to the legislation. Not by wilful, immediate decisions, but by gradual law-creation. Industry and the economy should be changed only within the framework of the legislative limits that are created. This is important not only because it will make reform non-reversible, but also because it will serve as a guarantee for the reforms, without which their authority will not grow and without which they will not be able to embrace all layers of the population.

During these years of independence a broad legislative framework, based on internationally adopted juridical principles and standards, and proceeding from the priority of human rights and freedoms, has been created in the Republic. We have taken a big step forward from the dictates and arbitrariness of the totalitarian system to legislative regulations covering citizens' relations with the state and also administrative-economic structures of all forms of property.

6. The sixth conclusion is that in determining the strategy and implementation of reforms it is necessary to pay special attention to the *links* that have defining significance in the renovation of society.

(i) *The transformations in the agrarian sector are the most significant in the whole chain of economic reforms.* The agrarian sector of the economy has mighty reserves today, the sensitive use of which can in the very near future bring palpable results.

The results of all our economic reforms, and indeed the stability and welfare of our population depend on how deep are the processes of radical transformation in the agricultural sector, and how far the reforms reach our villages. *The development of the market mechanism in villages and a revival of the feeling of ownership among farmers should take place by improving property relations, reorganizing state farms into economies based on preserving for farmers a viable farm property, rationalizing rent relations and providing land for lifelong use with the right to inherit.*

We have to create an agricultural economy that will provide an opportunity to every *dehkan* (farmer) to feel committed to remain working in this sector, to have a free hand in the distribution of produced goods and to provide his family with wealth. However, to release free working hands from the sphere of agriculture and to draw them into other spheres of the economy is the most important of our reforms in agriculture. *Agriculture in itself cannnot provide jobs for all the people who live in rural areas.* Over-manning results in obstacles in the development and reform of agriculture: slowing the implementation of high-level industrial methods of produc-tion with advanced tools of agrochemistry, and lowering labor productivity. But this is the economic side of the issue. There is also the social side. Reform means that many rural villagers, especially the young, have no chance of getting a job, and providing a proper life for themselves. This creates acute social problems in villages and is a potential threat to social stability. That is why the priority task for us is to create new work in the countryside by establishing small mobile enterprises equipped with modern technology.

We have given ourselves the task of creating fundamentally new structures in the villages – industrial and social infrastructure, communication nets, everyday life-enhancement services. If these services are properly organized, this will not only provide jobs for all who need them, but it will also essentially change the image of villages and their cultural life. This will contribute to the stabilization of public and political life in the country.

(ii) The structural transformations of our economy are being undertaken to provide economic independence for our Republic. The previous economy, which we inherited, was based on the interests of the former USSR. It met the interests of Soviet conditions of labor distribution and Uzbekistan was given its own role of 'raw material accessory'. Thus a prime task in our domestic policy is the decisive overcoming of this one-sided, directed economy of a provider of raw materials, which was limited by the narrow frames of past Soviet specialization.

For many years the Republic's economy was a small part of a unified public economy that was ruled from the center. Most of the decisions that were adopted there were far from the interests of Uzbekistan. *The Republic was the supplier of cheap raw materials and strategic mineral resources, and a 'capacities market' for the selling to the USSR of market-ready products.* Enterprises worked not to enrich domestic Republican markets, but to export products – products that passed away from their source. *The huge natural capacity of the Republic was exploited, but the profits passed beyond its borders.* Even today in many branches of industry the production of non-finished technological cycles is dominating. It breaks at the stage of the initial processing of raw materials and at the manufacture of half-finished products. This situation puts the economy of the Republic in a vulnerable position and threatens its stable development.

The independence of the Republic puts entirely new demands on the structural design of the economy. Structural transformations are a difficult, laborious and long process. Our structural policy will proceed from the demands of the market economy, taking into account the fact that the market requires entirely new forms of the division of labor, based on the principles of (a) high legal efficiency and (b) profit. Improving the territorial structure of our economy will allow the maximum and effective use of huge unclaimed resources and economic possibilities, and the to elimination of territorial disproportions.

Structural changes in the economy will first of all be directed at solving the problems of the deeper processing of agricultural raw materials and mineral resources, to increase the degree of the technological cycle. It is especially important in these processes to provide a breakthrough to advanced technologies, to a modern structure of production that sets up an interrelated system for the processing of raw mineral resources.

Of no less importance is the task to make our economy, and in particular our consumer market, less vulnerable to external destabilizing factors. Did it meet the interests of the nation, when in spite of our favorable natural and climatic environment we actually had to import all our sugar, baby food, grain, meat, cooking oil, dairy products, potatoes? We had to import even such elementary everyday items as matches and salt. That is why supplying the Republic with necessary goods, primarily through our own production, is an issue of both economic and political importance.

We aim to ensure that what we produce enters not only the domestic market but also the world market. The possession of modern technology and modern industrial management will be mediated through the creation of joint international ventures. To strengthen exports and to find markets for our best products in the face of severe competition, we need partners in reliable and strong foreign firms.

Our economy, based on a stable legislative framework and institutional reforms, is stage-by-stage entering the market economy, and becoming steady. The results of the years up to 1996 show this.

1. *Macroeconomic stability has been achieved as the main result of the reform of our entire economy.* The main economic indices (GDP, volume of industrial production, production of consumer goods, stable minimized level of state budget deficit, double annual reduction of level of inflation) all confirm that progress is being made.

2. *Our own national monetary system has almost been completed.* Measures directed at strengthening our national currency have been taken. This has allowed the strengthening of its role as a single means of payment. The organizational and legal conditions for the development of an out-of-exchange currency market have been created. Sufficient and stable gold currency reserves, which allow the holding of auctions at the Uzbek Republican Currency Exchange, have been accumulated.

3. *A wide market infrastructure has been formed.* New banking, financial and tax systems have been created, as well as stock, goods and raw materials exchanges, and insurance, auditing and leasing companies. The basis for the wide functioning of a securities market is being put in place. The largest financial exchange centre in Central Asia, equipped with modern computer technology and telecommunication systems, has been put into operation.

4. *The scale of privatization has been deepened and expanded.* At present, as a result of reforms, 70% of all employees involved in the national economy work in the private sector, along with 53.5% of employees in industry manufacturing and 97.7% of employees in agricultural production. But privatization is not for the sake of privatization, but in order to find real owners for property, to put it into the hands of people who are able to work, who fully comprehend the requirements of modern organizational management, who can attract investment and provide quality products.

5. *Entirely new branches of industry, such as automobile construction, microbiology and cellulose-paper have been created.* These new branches not only change the appearance of our economy, but also promote its independence from external threat and upset and help to increase both the gross domestic product and the standard of living of the population.

6. *The mentality of our people is changing and they are adapting to the changed standards of life.* Our achievements in the political, economic and social-cultural spheres are positively reflected in the social psychology of our citizens.

The uncertainty and confusion that existed in people's minds because of changes that flooded them have now disappeared. Today broad strands of the population are gradually adapting themselves to economic realities, and beginning to participate in the processes of the reform of all aspects of life in our society. All the changes that have occurred in the motivations of the citizens of Uzbekistan encourage us to conclude that, in terms of a positive and irreversible 'new mentality', a great change has taken place. The solid foundations for the stable and sustainable development of the Republic and for its security have been laid.

Chapter Twelve

Developing a strong social policy, and encouraging the growth of an active citizenry

During the period of shaping the national state system, implementing democratic reforms, transforming the economy and making the transition to market relations, special attention should be paid to social problems. This is the experience of the social development of many countries in the world, and the witness of the newly independent ex-Soviet states during their periods of reform. History teaches that social problems and contradictions assume an acute character, and serve as a potential threat to national security, civil peace and stability just when one social structure is replaced by another.

What are the reasons for this? What are the main causes that dictate the need to pay special attention to issues of social stability during the transition period? The most important among them, in my opinion, are the following:

1. Social contradictions have always been a moving force in political, social and economic transformations. The nature of these changes depends on how acute are these accumulated social problems and on how the governing structures can solve them – social protests, spontaneous explosions, right up to civil wars and revolutions.

2. We must pay attention to the 'social motivation' of the public. A human being is by nature a social entity, and that is why it is very important that he and his talents as an individual in society should be taken into account during the period of reforms. His understanding of the meaning and goals of the reforms must coincide with real results.

The provision of a free life, of the well-being of our people, of the conditions for a person to realise his possibilities – this is our task during the reform and renovation of our society. A return to the old totalitarian, ideology-driven command-distributive system that had a wage-leveling approach and lacked a sound basis to stimulate labor is of course not acceptable to us.

If we take into account that, during the transition period, in order to complete our ultimate goal – the democratization of society and the implementation of a free market economy – it has been necessary to take unpopular and sometimes even radical decisions that may at certain stages threaten the well-being of the population, then the importance of measures to support socially vulnerable groups of the population in order to assuage their pain becomes obvious. We have to be on the watch for bureaucratic infringement of the essentials of the reforms, violation of social equity, and corruption in government that aggravates the already hard life of the people.

The people's pain serves as a good soil in which to grow nostalgia for days gone by. This soil feeds various movements of different shades – from reactionary national-patriotic to liberal-socialist. A continual incitement, with mercenary and narrow-minded political motives, of a mood of social dissatisfaction in the public can only threaten civil peace and security.

3. The initial stage in the process of long-term, large-scale reforms I would define as the most difficult and socially explosive. This is not only because the transitional period is characterized by a multiplicity of unsolved social problems and carries with it a huge 'social charge', but also because the transition from one political and economic system to another produces new problems and bears definite social costs.

The transition to a market economy, as the experience of many countries shows, does not happen without the growth of social problems. The liberalization of the economy, especially the 'shock' release of consumer prices and tariffs, the decrease in production, the 'non-payment crisis', and the changes in money circulation, has resulted in a sharp increase in consumer prices, a devaluation of deposits, a reduction in the standard of living for a large part of the population, and the growth in the number of fully or partially unemployed people. Inadequate attention to social security at this period may cause – and we can see that this has happened in many countries – the impoverishment of a great part of the population: their lumpenization, which serves as a rich soil for social instability.

4. For many people the breaking of their usual way of living, the change of the stereotypes of thought and social behavior and the eradication of 'dependency patterns' may become an acute social problem. During the transition period a change in people's psychology takes place, and we know this is never painless. About three generations of people in the former USSR were educated on ideological dogmas; they rejected concepts of private property, had no skills in independent economic activity, and were educated on an ideology based on the concepts of the central-distribution system and a false understanding of the concept of social equity.

Inequality creates the danger of social instability in any country. The acuteness of this problem is not in somebody's being poor or rich, but in a big gap between these two groups. If society consists of groups of people with diametrically opposed views and aspirations, then there is always a danger of social unrest and thus of a threat to national security. Extreme social contradictions may lead to internal confrontations and even to civil wars.

That is why the most important task of the democratic state in the transition period is to neutralize acute social contradictions, to alleviate the inevitable difficulties of this period by adopting preventative measures and accommoding people to a new social environment. This is one of the most important advantages of Uzbekistan's policy in comparison with other states that are implementing the transition to a market economy.

The state that can find solutions to difficult questions such as how to ensure a social consensus and how to reach public agreement regarding international harmony can expect the stable progress of democratic and economic development. The provision of social agreement entails the achieving of that level of development at which social contradiction and inequity do not exceed the level beyond which there appear sections of the population who consider themselves to be unfairly deprived or limited in their rights. *That is why one of the leading principles on which the independence and renovation of Uzbekistan is based is the implementation of an effective social policy.*

The provision of reliable social guarantees and measures for the social protection of the population is a priority at all stages of market reform and penetrates other areas of the total renovation process in society. When we speak about the priority of the system of social protection, we first of all imply that the construction of a market economy is not an end in itself for us. The meaning and goal of the reforms is to create the necessary conditions for each citizen of Uzbekistan, irrespective of his national identity, belief and convictions, to prove himself as an effective personality, to reveal his skills and talent, and to make his life spiritually richer.

During the years of independence an entirely new mechanism of social protection has been created that takes into account the real economic situation, the available resources and possibilities. At the same time, we proceeded from the fact that various stages of reform must correspond to a thorough-going social policy.

In the deepening of reform and in the advancement to market priorities of social policy, measures of social protection and support will change. A wide choice of approaches and devices to regulate social policy has been used at various stages, including direct cash payments in the form of regularly revised wages, pensions, stipends, allowances, indirect payments, benefits, compensation payments, grants and subsidies.

In the initial stage of reform we followed the policy of *social protection of the entire population*. This played a significant role in preventing a sharp decrease in the standard of living, and provided quietness and stability in the Republic. During the first years of the reforms, the system of consumer subsidies and different forms of the protection of consumer markets against the diverting of main food items outside the country was widely used as a protective measure. This was an emergency action. Its necessity was determined by our wish to protect the consumer capacities of the population in the context of liberalized prices.

Measures have been taken to protect and support large and vulnerable families, the unemployed, individuals with limited savings, the newly-married and students, including such social incentives as free breakfasts for primary schools and lonely pensioners, free food for children under the age of two and for pregnant women with anaemia, and incentive food for schoolchildren and students. Subsidies for communal social services, and public electric transport have also been introduced.

Thanks to these approaches Uzbekistan – a country with most unfavorable starting conditions on the eve of reform and with palpable social contradictions – managed to escape social confrontation. At the same time, a deep analysis of the implemented reform measures of social protection revealed deficiencies, primarily due to wastefulness and a rooted dependency psychology. Grants and incentives were equally distributed among the population, irrespective of the degree of need for these incentives. This sometimes resulted in the use of benefits by families that did not need them.

That is why when the reforms went deeper and market relations expanded, there were introduced essential corrections to social policy. The emphasis was put on providing help to really needy families. Much work has been done to develop and implement a mechanism of targeted social protection of the population. The entire system of social support has been directed at doing away with wage-leveling and a dependency psychology. All allowances and material assistance were provided only through a family and the main receivers were vulnerable families, old people and children. The distinctive feature of the new system of social protection is the differentiated approach to various groups of the population.

The further improvement of the social protection of the population and its value for money are related to the solution of the following important tasks:

1. *The stabilization and steady development of production.*

It was possible in the initial stages of reform not to allow a sharp decrease in the standard of living due to the implementation of anti-inflation measures, the speedy development of the production of consumer goods, the strengthening of the national currency and the creation of a domestic consumer market.

Infant mortality has been reduced, life expectancy has increased, and crime has been reduced (its level is the lowest in the CIS). The stabilization of the economy, active investment processes, and support for small and middle business have created favorable ground for new work-places, solving employment issues and sharply reducing the number of part-time workers and those who are forced into holidays without salaries or with partially paid salaries.

Today Uzbekistan, thanks to the stable development of the economy, has the CIS's lowest level of unemployment, in spite of the fact that it is a country with a complicated demography, where employment issues were always very acute. We are planning to implement further policies of providing work-places by means of further structural reorganization of the economy, creating small production-units, first of all in rural areas, and stimulating the further development of small, private businesses.

2. *Of great importance, alongside state resources, are the assets of working collectives and social and charity organizations.*

In the implementation of social assistance to the population, the rights and responsibility of local government should be significantly expanded. Local government can introduce additional measures of social support depending on the possibilities in their regions. A prime task of local government is to create realistic possibilities for work.

3. *The development of a powerful motivation mechanism that can provide the full activization of the labour and the skills of the people.*

First of all, by creating conditions that will provide the combination of economic freedom for each person and his economic responsibility for his prosperity and the prosperity of his family. Through such a combination will an individual's own skills and labor be the most stable source of prosperity. It is thus important to speed up the development of the institution of private property. The adaptation to the 'market reality' will provide a significant part of the aggregated revenues of the population from business activity and property profits.

4. *The repudiation of an unjustifiably high level of differentiation in the profits and standard of living of the population, and the creation of an acceptable stratification in society that will provide social stability.*

The socially-protective measures that were undertaken prevented the possibility of the development of a sharp differentiation within the population depending on their profits. Today the gap between the revenues of the well-supplied group of the population and the revenues of the less-supplied group has been reduced to 7.5 times (the threshold being 8 times). Any increase will signal a serious social differentiation.

5. *The struggle against poverty; the strengthening of state support to the vulnerable parts of the people.*

One of the main evils in any society is poverty. None of the countries of the world, even the richest, has been able to escape it. It is not surprising that the General Assembly of UN announced 1996 as the International Year of the Eradication of Poverty. During our transition period to a market economy, the problem of poverty raises its head even more acutely. This is because today some of those who have never been considered poor but were among the middle and upper-middle classes are joining the category of poor people.

In solving the problem of eradicating poverty, the so-called 'vulnerable groups' of the population, including invalids, single mothers, orphans, and old people deserve special attention. However, the social support provided here must have a clear-cut, targeted direction.

The corner-stone of our social policy is an orientation to the social support of the family. We place great emphasis on increasing the role of the family in strengthening the social foundations of our state, its stability and the education of a physically-healthy, spiritually-rich young generation, on whom the fate of our country will depend tomorrow. We are forging (a) powerful guarantees to protect motherhood and childhood, (b) reforms in the educational sphere and in the professional training of the growing generation, and (c) different social funds are being created to support and strengthen families and to provide them with financial support. Lately a new form of allowances has been introduced that is targeted only at vulnerable groups of the population, *through families*.

Taking into account our specific national mentality and way of living, such a form of social support as selection of the less protected families and providing them with help through *mahalla* committees is used today. This approach has centuries-old roots. The present way of living of our people demands the targeted distribution of assets assigned to support socially dependent, needy groups of the population. Our new mechanism for providing support for families takes full account of and uses national traditions of mutual support.

Summing up, I would like to stress that the special importance in all these issues is the increase of the political activity of the people. This can happen if we provide our citizens with a wide range of rights and freedoms, and stimulate their active participation in the public and political life of our society. It is very important that all persons feel themselves citizens of their country, value the rights and freedoms offered to them, and appreciate and defend the values of democracy that have been gained through our hard work.

In the increase of the democratic communal activity of people, in the solution of the many ripe problems of our polity, the role of social non-state structures is important. If we lack a clear-cut understanding of this, if we lack a strong consensus about the structures of our society, we will not have reliable guarantees against the manifestations on all levels of relapses into subjective approaches and violations of the principles of social equity.

When we begin to evaluate the current social reality in the Republic from this point of view, we can say that the most difficult tests that our people faced and were inevitable in the transition period are already behind us. Everything connected with narrow-mindedness and ideological blindness has gone into the past. The feeling of participation in every event taking place not only in the country but also beyong its borders is growing. A certain bitter experience, accumulated during the years of independence, and the knowledge of the experience of other countries, has opened our eyes, and we have become more wise and tolerant. New horizons of spirituality, morality and culture, and the possibility of the recreation of our wonderful national traditions are spread before us.

Today there are no factors that could negatively affect the material well-being of our people. On the contrary, stabilizing factors are gaining more speed and creating conditions and reliable guarantees for the growth of people's standard of living. But the most important thing is that the mentality and outlook of the people are changing, and their political and social consciousness is growing. Today we are not the same as we were six years ago. I am convinced that nothing can shift our people with such an attitude from their chosen road.

Chapter Thirteen

Geostrategic potential, resources of natural and raw material

In the modern world each country, including the Republic of Uzbekistan, is not an isolated territory, but part of a complex of geographical and political systems with world-wide economic links.

Uzbekistan is located between the Amudarya and the Syrdarya rivers and has a favorable geostrategic situation, from the point of view of establishing international links and of the prospects for their development. From ancient times the Great Silk Road connecting East and West passed through the territory of Uzbekistan. Many trade routes converged here. An intensive process of external contacts and the mutual enrichment of various cultures took place here. Today too routes from Europe and the Middle East to the Asian-Pacific region cross here.

These links acquired a special importance and dynamic when the Central Asian countries gained independence and sovereignty. This is not surprising. The territories of the Central Asian countries stretch from the borders of China in the east up to Iran and the Caspian Sea in the west and connect the Indian subcontinent with Russia and Europe. The importance of Uzbekistan and other Central Asian republics in the modern geopolitical system is so great that events occurring in our republics directly touch the interests of the world's largest powers and of various geopolitical formations. In forming its geopolicy, any state must take into account this circumstance, and seek to obtain for itself political, economic and strategic advantages.

Thus the territorial peculiarities of Uzbekistan and its geographical situation are important in deciding and implementing our internal and external policies. Occupying the central geopolitical situation in Central Asia, Uzbekistan has every opportunity to play a central role in the processes of the maintenance of the balance of forces, and in the creation of a solid basis for co-operation, in this strategically important region, which already today, on the threshold of the twenty-first century, has acquired a special significance on the political and economic map of the world by virtue of its actual and potential natural and raw resources.

Uzbekistan, being today the most socially and economically advanced country in the region, has enormous cultural potential, serving as a link between the neighboring states of Kazakhstan, Kyrgyzstan, Tajikistan, Turkmenistan and Afghanistan. Through the active co-operation with Uzbekistan on the part of the international community an opportunity to establish a fraternal polity all over the Central Asian region has opened up.

Being the core of Central Asia, Tashkent serves, metaphorically speaking, as the gateway to the East. Appreciating this, the delegations and offices of many international organizations, such as the United Nations, the International Monetary Fund, the World Bank, the European Bank for Reconstruction and Development, the Organization for Security and Co-operation in Europe, the German Society for Technical Assistance and many others have been opened in Tashkent. The representative offices of more than 350 foreign organizations, companies and banks have their accreditation in Uzbekistan. All this opens opportunities for the Republic to be integrated into the world economy, to attract foreign investment, and to be transformed into a regional center for mutually advantageous interstate co-operation, the transit of goods and capital, and the development of transport, tourist and financial services.

Here it is necessary to mention our unique natural and raw material potential. Our favorable climate, huge mineral and agricultural material resources, and large stocks of strategic materials place Uzbekistan among the richest countries of the region and the world. On the map of the world there are few states that own as much wealth as Uzbekistan. A large part of this is untapped and this fact cannot but attract the attention of international companies and banks.

Uzbekistan is rightfully proud of the richness of its land — in fact all the elements in Mendeleev's periodic system are found here. Today more than 2,700 deposits and promising signs of the ore of different kinds of minerals, including about a hundred types of mineral raw material have been detected, of which more than 60 are already under utilization. More than 900 deposits have been prospected where the confirmed stocks are estimated at US$970 billion. Thus it is necessary to note that the overall potential of mineral and raw material resources is estimated at more than US$3.3 trillion.

Concerning such major strategic resources as oil and gas condensate and natural gas, 155 promising deposits have been prospected; precious metals — more than 40; non-ferrous, rare and radioactive metals — 40; mineable-chemical raw material — 15. Thus the current level of discovered deposits of metals, fuel resources, minerals and raw materials for building are a good basis for optimism about the future of the Republic.

Annually minerals worth US$5.5 billion are extracted, and new stocks worth US$6–7 billion have been detected. In relation to such important minerals as gold, uranium, copper, tungsten, potash salt, phosphorites, and kaolin, Uzbekistan, by virtue of its confirmed stocks and prospected ores, occupies a leading position not only within the CIS but also in the world. The Republic ranks 4th in the world in terms of its gold stocks, and 7th in terms of the level of output. In copper stocks it ranks 10th–11th, in uranium 7th–8th.

The existing and exploited stocks of raw mineral materials in most cases not only provide work for mining complexes for a long period, but also allow the increase of production capacities for the extraction of a number of strategic minerals. Already now the production of raw mineral material and its processing is one of the leading sectors in the economy of the Republic, and one that exerts great influence on the development of industry and agriculture. On the basis of the prospected stocks about 400 mines, pitfalls and oil and gas fields are under operation.

The developed deposits of minerals in the Republic differ from those in other CIS countries not only in their large amounts, but also in a number of other particularities, among which I want to specify the following.

1. Natural and mineral raw material resources are concentrated in large deposits, and there is the possibility of processing them comprehensively right at the area of their extraction.
2. Many kinds of minerals have not only a high content of usable essential material, but also a great variety of accompanying elements.
3. A large part of the deposits can be processed openly using a comprehensive but simple technology of enrichment with ores, which ensures a high degree of extraction of these products, which are much in demand on the world market.
4. Many mineral deposits are located in well-populated areas, with good transport access and the means of inter-territorial displacement of resources, including pipeline transport for liquid and gas.
5. The nation is able to provide the necessary industrial and social infrastructure, along with a qualified staff in higher and secondary specialized institutions that train specialists for the mining industries.

It would be impossible to give an assessment of the whole spectrum of mineral and raw material resources available in the Republic within the framework of this book. I would like only to focus attention on those resources that have a crucial strategic importance for the Republic's independence and economic power.

First. Uzbekistan has a unique stock of fuel and energy resources. The prospected stocks of gas make up about 2 trillion cubic meters, and coal more than 2 billion tons. More than 160 deposits of oil are exploitable.

The stocks of oil, gas and condensate not only meet our own needs completely, but are also available for export. Today this energy sector is one of the most profitable areas in which to invest capital.

Experts estimate that there are huge undiscovered oil and gas deposits in Uzbekistan — that about 60 per cent of the Republic's territory is promising for the extraction of these energy resources.

Five basic oil and gas fields may be listed in the following regions: Usturt, Bukhara-Khiva, South-Western Gissar, Surkhan-Darya and Ferghana. The stocks of oil and gas resources are estimated to be worth more than US$1 trillion.

The prospected stocks will meet the Republic's needs in natural gas for more than 35 years and in oil for 30 years. More than 90 per cent of oil is extracted by the gushing method, which is considered to be cheaper.

In 1992 in Namangan province the promising Mingbulak region oilfield was discovered, and its industrial operation will enable Uzbekistan to meet completely its demand for oil and petroleum products.

Special attention should be paid to the fact that the deposits of petroleum and gas in Uzbekistan have a number of particularities, including the efficiency of chinks and extraction costs, which are very advantageous in comparison with the deposits in neighboring regions, and which will allow us to rely on their effective development and high profitability. At the same time, additional expenses in the extracting of these stocks of oil will be relatively low, because in this case there is no need to create the infrastructure for their extraction, preparation and transportation.

Another distinctive feature is that the degree of exhaustion of the prospected oil stocks in Uzbekistan makes up only 32 per cent, whereas this parameter in Turkmenistan is 61 per cent, in Kyryzstan 41 per cent, and in Tajikistan 60 per cent. A similar situation is observed with regard to our natural gas reserves.

All these factors and the availability of a developed infrastructure make Uzbekistan a favourable bet in terms of investment and development.

There are great prospects for the Republic in the development of the gas extraction industry, related to the processing of natural gas and gas condensate.

Our largest gas deposits are located in the South-Western Gissar region and in the Bukhara-Khiva oilfield and gasfield regions, namely the Shurtan and Mubarek areas.

In the composition of the extracted gases there are ethane, propane, butane and other components, suitable for the obtaining of polymeric materials: polyethylene, polyvinylchloride and others. Besides, propane from the Shurtan gas and chemical complex can be used to obtain nitryl-acrilic acid, with the further manufacturing of nitron fiber.

The utilization of sulphur compounds is stipulated in all the operational and projected enterprises related to gas and gas condensate processing.

In recent years, there have been truly dynamic developments in the oil and gas processing industries. There are two oil refineries (in Ferghana and Altyaryk) and two gas processing plants (in Shurtan and Mubarek) in operation in the territory of the Republic, producing a wide range of oil and gas derivatives. During the years of independence the production of such new kinds of products as petrol, kerosene for planes, petrol for planes, various kinds of oil lubricants and liquid gas was embarked on. Today the Republic has ceased importing crude oil and many kinds of oil and petroleum products. And with the Bukhara oil refinery in operation we shall not only be fully able to meet the national demand for oil products, but able also considerably to expand our exports of these products.

Uzbekistan has large stocks of coal, and occupies second place in Central Asia in this respect. Coal extraction takes place in Uzbekistan at three deposit-sites: Angren, Shargun and Baisun with the total amount of 2 billion tonnes.

Among them the Angren coal deposit is considered to be unique. Here the extraction of coal is conducted in a progressive and economically expedient way: by an open method when the depth of coal layers is 150–250 meters, by an underground method, and by using the method of underground gasification. In addition, modern methods of non-waste technology are being used.

Along with coal, the extraction of what are judged to be the most valuable mineral and raw-material resources is also being carried on and developed: kaolin, limestone, quartz sand, pebbles and some rare elements, all of which adds up to a sufficient raw material base from which to develop many kinds of new manufacturing.

Kaolin is of great interest in industrial development. Kaolin from the Angren region can be used in many industries as a raw material from which to obtain alumina and aluminum, fire-proof materials, ceramic facing, porcelain and faience, electro-isolators, drainage and canalization tubes, fill-ins in paper industry, white and colored cement, highly resistant bricks and much else. A good raw material, a well-developed area, the availability of free plots of land, water and human resources, electrical and thermal energy, railways with terminals and an international airport provide reliable prospects for the establishment of an industrial complex to manufacture crushed and enriched kaolin. The first stage is the construction of a factory to produce enriched kaolin and alumina. Preliminary calculations have shown a high efficiency of investment, and its recoupment within 4 (for kaolin) and 7 (for alumina) years respectively.

Second. *Uzbekistan is among those countries possessing the largest resources of gold, silver and other precious and rare metals in the world.*

To date there are 40 deposits of precious metals. The major stocks of gold are concentrated fundamentally in gold ore deposits in Central Kyzylkums. By stocks, the Republic ranks fourth in the world.

The deposits in Muruntau are among the world's giants, being among the largest known in the Eurasian continent, and having a high content of gold in the ore. The Muruntau deposit has been recognized by the international geological community as the greatest discovery of the second half of the twentieth century in the field of gold. The open pit of Muruntau is a huge bowl, from which millions of cubic meters of mountain mass are annually extracted. This facilitates the extracting of the best gold in the world. This in itself is a unique example for the gold mining industry of the world. Sophisticated technology for purifying the gold has been introduced in affinage production, by a number of techniques, allowing the obtaining of gold of 'four nine' purity and of a magnificent commodity finish, which has already brought to Uzbekistan numerous international rewards.

Over many years of Muruntau's operation large amounts of mineralized mass with 'extra-balance sheet' contents of gold for industrial reprocessing were sorted out and stockpiled at the Muruntau open pit. Today, with the participation of the USA's Newmont Mining Corporation, they are being reprocessed using the most advanced technologies.

In recent years gold ore deposits have been detected in the Samarkand and Tashkent regions, both of which have a highly developed infrastructure. Alongside Muruntau, which is located in the Kyzylkum and is the largest gold ore province in the world, new deposits in Adjibugut, Bulutkan, Balpantau, Aristantau, and Turbai have been detected and are now being explored.

The distinctive feature of all the gold ore deposits and industries in the Kyzylkum zone is a high content of gold in the ore, an open method of extraction and the availability of engineering networks and communications (water, gas, electric power, railroads and highways).

The Republic has pure silver deposits. These are the Vysokovoltnoye, Okjetpes and Kosmonachy deposits in the Navoi region, and the Aktepa deposit in the Namangan region. Moreover, a considerable amount of these stocks also contain gold and copper-porphyritic deposits. The deposit in Aktepa is the most promising for the extraction of silver and the most attractive for the involvement of foreign investment.

In addition to precious metals, Uzbekistan also produces uranium, for which a large mineral and raw material infrastructure-base has been created. The prospected stocks of uranium are sufficient for its production for 50–60 years. Being produced alongside uranium, such valuable materials as rhenium, scandium and lantanoids are extracted. The overwhelming majority of such materials in one way or another pass into a productive solution of lixiviation. The introduction of the newest extraction technology could in this case considerably increase the efficiency of the processing of these deposits.

Third. *Uzbekistan has significant prospected stocks of non-ferrous metals; including copper, lead, zinc, tungsten and other metals of this group.*

Our copper ores have compacted with them more than 15 kinds of non-ferrous metals, such as gold, silver, molybdenum, cadmium, indium, tellurium, selenium, rhenium, cobalt, nickel and osmium. It is a characteristic feature that the extraction of these ores is predominantly carried out by an open method, thus ensuring the profitability of the mines. The operating open pits are capable of supplying copper and the accompanying metals for 40–50 years, and zinc and lead for more than 100 years.

The stocks of ores of *non-ferrous metals* are predominantly concentrated in the Almalyk ore field. The Kalmakyr deposit is uniquely large, exceeding considerably its analogues abroad in the production of copper-molybdenum ores. The ore processing of this deposit is carried out by the Almalyk mining and smelting plant, which is one of the largest enterprises in Uzbekistan.

A promising copper deposit in Dalney, with large stocks of copper, molybdenum, gold, silver, rhenium, tellurium, selenium and sulphur has been prospected. In the exploitation of the Dalney deposit, which is to be carried out with the participation of foreign capital, to extract copper and its accompanying metals, the construction of a new concentrating mill has been suggested. If the mill is built, it will be provided with raw ore material that will last for 200 years. The Dalney deposit, according to the prospected stocks, to the price of its extraction, to the degree of the successful extraction of the minerals, is a unique one, having no similar analogues in the CIS countries.

Lead and zinc deposits are mainly concentrated in Uchkulach in the Jizak region and in Khandiza in the Surkhan Darya region. In the Khandiza deposit, copper, silver, cadmium, selenium, gold and indium have also been detected. With the growth in demand for these metals on the international markets, the expansion of their extraction will become desirable in Uzbekistan.

With investment for the technical and technological re-equipment of the existing production facilities, it will be possible to obtain the rare metals that are extracted in the processing of copper ores of superior quality, containing 99.99 per cent of the basic metal. We have a reliable raw material base for the extraction and production of a number of rare and fissile metals. Some of them are concentrated in separate, independent deposits, as for example lithium, but others can be extracted as accompanying components from copper, polymetals and uranium.

The utilization of selenium and tellurium is mainly connected with the manufacture of semiconductors, solar batteries, thermo-generators and special brands of steel and glass.

Uzbekistan has unique stocks of rhenium, which is inside the copper ores of the Almalyk deposits. They have no analogues in the world as far as the amount of rhenium in our molybdenum concentrates is concerned. Rhenium is widely used in industry to manufacture heat-resistant alloys for aircraft, spacecraft, electronic devices, and catalysts for the cracking of oil.

In Africa, Switzerland and Russia there are available natural sources of rhenium in which the presence of the isotype osmium 187 is only 1.6 per cent, while in the copper-molybdenum ores of the Uzbek deposits that contain rhenium the percentage of a stable isotope of osmium is much higher.

The feasibility of obtaining products containing osmium on an industrial basis is strengthened by the presence in our country of large stocks of the appropriate initial raw material, exceeding by three times the deposit in Norilsk in Russia.

Fourth. *20 deposits of marble, and 15 of granite and gabbro have been explored in the Republic.* Many deposits of decorative stone, varying in color from white through all the colors of the rainbow to black, constitute a unique natural treasure, and are among the largest in the entire Eurasian zone. The total stocks of our decorative stone exceed 85 mllion cubic meters, enough to provide our stone-processing industry with raw material for hundreds of years. With such a powerful raw material base, Uzbekistan is one of the leaders in stone processing among the CIS countries.

There are also the possibilities of using the wonderful qualities of our natural decorative stone in modern construction on a large scale, and of exporting our marble and granite products. There are projects to create enterprises with the participation of foreign partners for the production of stone building blocks, using the most modern technology by exploiting the Gazgan, Nurata and Zarband deposits, which have the necessary communications and engineering networks. Calculations show that financial recoupment in the cases of these projects will be within two years.

Fifth. *The Republic is rich in phosphorites.* Forecasts of the prospected stocks of small grain phosphorites of the Morocco type in the Jeroy-Sardar phosphoric deposit are about 100 million tons. The construction of the Kyzylkum phosphoric plant is now underway to produce 2.7 million tons of phosphoric concentrate. Further, the Karakat deposit has been preliminarily explored, and the Northern

Jetutau deposit has been assessed, both of which are also located in Central Kyzylkum. Forecast phosphorite stocks, according to geologists' statements, are actually unlimited.

The involvement of phosphorites in the economic life of the country arises because the capacity to manufacture phosphate fertilizers – ammophos superphosphates – have been created. However, our prospected deposits of phosphorites with stocks of about 300 million tons are yet to be exploited. With the purpose of increasing the export potential of manufactured phosphate fertilizers, and taking into account the availability of significant stocks of phosphorites, there is an opportunity to set up production facilities for their enrichment on the basis of the Karakatin and Northern Jetutau deposits with the participation of foreign investors.

Sixth. *There are large deposits of potash salts in Uzbekistan*, in Tyubegatan in the Kashkadarya region and in *Khojaikan* in the Surkhan Darya region. Our potash salt deposits are forecast to last for more than 100 years.

Exploiting the Tyubegatan potash salt deposit, the production of potash fertilizers is to go ahead with the participation of foreign investors. The further processing of these salts allows us also to obtain bromides, fermium, magnesite and gypsum.

Seventh. *The Republic has rich deposits of rock salt.* Forecasts show that five deposits of rock salt – Khodjaikan, Tubegatan, Barsakelmes, Baibichekan and Akkalin – amount to more than 90 billion tons. At the moment, salts of the Barsakelmes deposit are planned to be used as the raw material for the production of calcium and caustic soda, with the participation of foreign investors. For this purpose the the construction of the Kungrad soda plant for the production of calcium and caustic soda by chemical methods has begun.

The current situation of our mineral raw material base not only requires the full capacities of the existing mining and processing enterprises, but also creates favorable preconditions for the construction of new production-plants for gold, silver, copper, kaolin, fluorspar, phosphorous and potash fertilizers. As world experience shows, investment directed at the development of highly solvent minerals brings in big revenues. The world's leading foreign companies are today already actively participating with us in this development.

1. In 1992 the first Uzbek–US joint venture for gold production 'Zarafshan–Newmont', was set up, the founder of which was the American company Newmont Mining Corporation. This venture was set up to extract gold from the mineralized mass wastes of the Muruntau open pit. The construction of a mill, the cost of which was more than UK$220 million, was begun in October 1993 and finished in May 1995. In 1995 the joint venture produced its first gold.

2. In 1994 a joint Uzbek–British enterprise, Amantau Goldfields, was created, the foreign founders of which were the Lonrho Company (Great Britain) and the International Financial Corporation. The goal of this venture is to develop the gold ore deposits in Daughiztau and Amantaitau. This plant is expected to start up in 1998.

3. An agreement has been signed between Uzbek partners and the prestigious companies Newmont Mining Corporation (USA) and Mitsui (Japan), aimed at developing gold ore deposits in the Tashkent zone.

A number of similar promising projects in many other areas are now being studied. The possibilities for Uzbekistan of mutually beneficial joint co-operation with foreign companies in the development of the natural wealth of the Republic are far from exhausted. The above examples of such co-operation prove once again how attractive such projects are for foreign investors.

Owing to the one-sided, distorted structure of our economy, inherited from the Soviet system, the Republic manufactures a wide assortment of semi-finished items. These products of primary processing and in some cases of a complete technological cycle can serve as good initial material for the manufacture of competitive final products.

Refined copper, produced in the Republic as a semi-finished item for the production of a wide assortment of cables that enjoy great demand on both world and domestic markets can serve as an example of such deep processing.

Kaprolactam is another most valuable semi-finished item. Unfortunately, only 10 per cent of the kaprolactam produced in the Republic is used today for further processing. Taking into account the use of kaprolactam worldwide, it will be expedient to undertake its deep processing here in the Republic. To meet this objective, there has arisen the opportunity to create a number of enterprises to manufacture kapron fibres and threads for further use in the manufacture of mixed fabrics, carpets, unwoven textiles and other such consumer goods.

Furthermore, during kaprolactam processing it is possible to obtain various construction plastics that are used in the automobile and aircraft industries and in a number of other industries, as manufacturing products for technical-industrial purposes. Apart from this, it is also possible to obtain film polyamides to manufacture packing materials, the demand for which is practically unlimited within and outside the Republic.

In order to use our raw material resources to their most productive extent, our task is to create processing facilities so that up to 70–80 per cent of the kaprolactam produced is used for further processing. This problem is to be solved by attracting foreign capital, by creating kapron thread factories, and by the subsequent organization of a number of light industrial enterprises to manufacture consumer goods, alongside a very substantial enterprise to produce construction plastics.

The industrial capacity to manufacture 23 thousand tons of *nitron fiber* has been created in the Republic. This production is the initial raw material for the fabrics for furniture, rugs, yarn for hand-operated and machine knitting, socks, stockings, carpets, needle thread, blankets, artificial fur and a great variety of other such fabrics. The processing of nitron fiber to achieve finished products is at present not more than 25 per cent of this industry's output, while the rest is exported in semi-finished form. Given the availability of the raw material resources for the manufacture of nitron fiber and given the great demand for it within and without the Republic, and also given the need to increase production efficiency, the reconstruction and expansion of the Navoi plant is scheduled for the near future.

Uzbekistan's rich, high soil fertility is enabling us to transform the Republic into a country with a powerful agro-industrial potential, which is one of our chief characteristics. Favorable climatic conditions and an irrigated agriculture have led to good conditions for the development of our historically-powerful agricultural base and of the manufacturing infrastructure for the processing of agricultural raw material.

Uzbekistan is a country of ancient irrigation. Irrigated agriculture is the basis of the Republic's self-reliance in food and a source for the production of exports. Today Uzbekistan is one of the primary producers and suppliers of a product of high financial liquidity on the international markets – cotton fiber. The Republic ranks fourth in the world for cotton fiber production and second for its export. Our course is the industrial-commercial development of the in-depth processing of cotton, so that it renders the maximum opportunities to create additional employment and revenue, and this course is being consistently pursued. Investment in our cotton processing, textile and sewing industries is among the most effective and profitable, yielding a rapid return.

Today in the four cities of Bukhara, Andijan, Tashkent and Ferghana large textile factories are in operation. In addition, over thirty yarn-weaving factories are located in various regions. Dozens of joint ventures with foreign investors, such as Kabul-Toytepa-Textiles (South Korea), Asnamtextile, Katex, Eltex, Samzhintex (Turkey), Supertextile (USA) have been created.

The Republic occupies a leading place among the CIS countries in the production of fruit, vegetables, silk cocoons, astrakhan and wool. Our excellent natural climatic conditions make it possible to obtain several harvests per year of potatoes and various other vegetables and crops. The use of our existing industrial base enables us to produce a wide variety of fresh and tinned fruit and vegetables, and in amounts that not only meet the demand of the Republic's population, but also provide for the population of many countries of the world. Today about 5 million tons of fruit and vegetables are produced annually, considerably in excess of the requirements of the domestic market.

However, it has to be said that shortages in modern refrigerating facilities and storehouses, and in compact and efficient enterprises for the processing of fruit and vegetables and the manufacture of packing materials, lead to great losses. Therefore the introduction of up-to-date technology for the processing, packing and marketing of fruit and vegetables is vitally necessary so that we might get a fast and high return.

Uzbekistan has long been famous for the high quality of its fruit and grapes. Such prized subtropical fruit as figs, pomegranates and persimmons are cultivated. We have the natural resources that lead to our strong capacities for the sale of fresh fruit outside the Republic. It is noteworthy that the fruits grown in the Republic are ecologically clean and contain a great variety of nutritious substances.

Of course, fresh grapes are the perfect raw material to make wines of high quality. Wine-makers in the Republic annually produce 16.5 million decaliters of wine materials (more than 30 brands of wine, various types of champagne and brandy). Uzbek wines have received awards on 92 occasions at international fairs, tastings, competitions and exhibitions.

The Republic has an immense potential to expand production in its silk industry, in its astrakhan breeding and in its tanning industry, using up-to-date technology.

The possession of huge mineral raw material and agricultural resources, much of which is unique and in great demand on world markets, not only makes Uzbekistan attractive for the establishment of mutually beneficial economic and trade relations, but also creates high desirable conditions for the formation, with interested foreign partners, of an advanced modern economy, which is able to ensure in the near and far future the sustainable and progressive development of the country, and a high level of prosperity for its people.

Chapter Fourteen

Human potential; social and industrial infrastructure

The hardworking, sympathetic and hospitable people of Uzbekistan are the genuine riches and wealth of their country.

Being society's superior value, the people bear a powerful potential, whose realization is serving as a mighty factor in the development of our society. Human potential is the most active, the most creative factor, ensuring a dynamic advancement of the country along the road of reforms and radical transformation. In its turn, the force and influence of this factor is determined by many other factors: for example the level of spirituality; the level of the economic and social development; the level of education; the structure of professional qualification; the level of employment.

The country's social and demographic situation plays a decisive role in the shaping of its human potential and its labor resources.

A high population growth rate is characteristic of Uzbekistan. It is sufficient to note that, although a decline of natural population growth can be traced over recent years, it still remains one of the highest among CIS countries. Between 1990 and 1996 the population of the country increased by 13.3 per cent. The annual average growth of the population was 2 per cent in 1996 or 450,000 people. Currently more than 23 million people live in the Republic, and that is far more than in the neighboring countries.

The strong institution of the family as the basis of society constitutes another distinctive social feature of our country. A high level of marriage is registered in Uzbekistan, which at the same time has the lowest level of divorce in the world. The family was and remains for our people an institution of vital value, a value that corresponds to our centuries-old traditions and indeed to our very mentality. Integrated families, when different generations live together and maintain a common household, are characteristic of the Republic. This creates favorable conditions for the education of children, and for their assimilation of universal spiritual values, and of our traditions. The virtues of hard work, the respect for elders, and a thirst for knowledge are nurtured in such families from early childhood.

In a social and economic context all this means that the Republic has a steady and intensive inflow of labor resources, and, as a result, good opportunities to establish labor-intensive enterprises and industrial branches of production.

Today the Republic has a powerful labor potential. Labor resources make up almost 50 per cent of the whole population and are growing by around 220,000 people every year. The age and professional structure of our labor potential also have distinctive features. The average age of the population in Uzbekistan is 24 years, which allows us on the eve of the 21st century to have a structure of labor resource which is characterized by high labor activity and professional training.

The structural redistribution of the employed population, i.e. the involvement of the younger generation who are entering their working age in new, desirable spheres of activity entails an effective utilization of our labor potential. Today over one-third of all our workers are involved in agriculture. Redistributing them into and retraining them for other spheres of the economy (first of all into the industrial and service sectors) opens a wide road to structural changes in the economy and its development.

That is why today one of the most important problems to be solved in the Republic is not only the provision of jobs for all people who want to work, but also the creation of the necessary conditions to create forms of employment that promote social harmony and improvement – the provision to every citizen of an opportunity freely to choose the type of work truly appropriate to him or her self.

A high educational level is a distinctive feature of the labor potential of Uzbekistan. We have almost completely solved the problem of the overall literacy of the population. The literacy rate is 99.06 per cent, and that places the Republic among the economically developed countries with a high level of development of human potential. It also has a high level of both the general and the professional training of its labor resources. Compulsory general secondary education is set out in the legislation of the Republic. It is realised through a wide network of comprehensive and specialist schools, vocational and technical colleges and business schools.

The statistical data on this subject is interesting and illustrative. For every 1,000 inhabitants of the age of 15 years and over, the number of people who have complete and incomplete higher education has substantially increased to the point when it is now 143 people. Years of training have now reached 11.4. 200 people for every 1,000 have a specialized secondary education. Every fourth worker employed in the sectors of material production and services has a higher or a specialized secondary education. In other words, in terms of its educational level the Republic belongs to the highly educated countries. This has become possible owing to the development of a wide, complex network of higher, secondary, specialized and vocational educational institutions, in accordance with our implementation of reforms in the educational system. Today this network comprises 59 centers of higher education and 258 secondary specialized educational institutions, including 75 colleges.

The core of our higher educational system is constituted by our major university centers, all widely known outside the Republic: Tashkent and Samarkand State Universities, the University of World Economy and Diplomacy, the University of World Languages, the Tashkent University of Economy, the Technical University, the Agrarian University, the Music Conservatoire, the Theater Institute, as well as a wide network of medical, technical, social-science and humanities higher education centers in all regions of the Republic.

Our establishments for the training, retraining and improving of the professional skills of the personnel constituting the executive bodies of state officials, and of the experts in the various domains of our economy, are the Academy of State and Public Construction, under the direction of the President of the Republic of Uzbekistan, and the Academy of Banking and Finance. Our training of experts in various fields of knowledge connected with the development of a market economy, advanced management methods and the scientific and technical development of production and external economic activity is expanding.

Today more than 360,000 students train and qualify in universities and vocational colleges. Great attention is being paid to expose our youth to the treasuries of world science, culture, education and knowledge. Links between the universities of the Republic and foreign educational centers have become stronger. The practice of inviting foreign professors and experts to lecture in foreign languages, as well as training employees and students abroad in universities and scientific centers, is growing. At the same time more than 1,250 foreign citizens from more than 40 countries of the world receive their education in Uzbekistan.

In this 'linking' sphere of education Uzbekistan has developed an active co-operation with such international organizations as ACCELS, IREX, the Consortium of American Colleges, CAPE, the Peace Corps (USA), DAAD, Konrad Adenauer Fund (Germany), British Council (UK), and the Saud-Al Baptine Fund (Egypt). Preparatory work is underway to establish Uzbek-American and Uzbek-Korean universities, as well as, jointly with partners from Canada, an International High School of Business and Management. The President of the Republic of Uzbekistan has established the 'Umid' Fund to support gifted young people in their studies abroad. This provides opportunities to study for bachelor's or master's degrees in many specializations at the most prestigious universities in the USA, Great Britain, France, Germany and Japan at the expense of our student grant system. All this is directed at the creation of an educated body of citizens who will form a basis for the powerful implementation of democratic and economic reforms in the country, thereby strengthening and increasing labor and intellectual potential.

The promotion of a research infrastructure for science and technology is of primary importance for the realization of our projected educational objectives. Our nation's scientific community holds a powerful intellectual potential that finds its practical application in many arenas of life, and serves as one of the bases for strengthening the state system and the economic independence of the Republic. So far as technology is concerned, the successful performance of enterprises is fundamentally predetermined today by the extent to which the very latest achievements of technological progress and research-related technologies are introduced, and also by the educational level of the personnel involved in both application and research.

Historically, circumstances have been such that, on the threshold of the twenty-first century, we possess a scientific potential which, in its level of development and innovation, is higher than that of many developing countries of the world, and in many respects is as high as that in the economically-developed countries. The foundations of the present flourishing of our scientific and general intellectual potential were laid down many centuries ago. We may say with pride that our national science dates back to very ancient times and has deep and powerful roots. For centuries it has reliably served the Uzbek nation and indeed the whole of mankind in revealing the secrets of nature and in pushing forward the frontiers of medicine, philosophy, law, theology, literature and linguistics.

Even in the distant past, distinguished Uzbek thinkers had intellectual successes and made scientific discoveries that are now incorporated into the treasury of universal culture and science. Our great ancestors whose names are well known all over the world stand at the origins of the treasury of knowledge. They include mathematicians and astronomers Al-Khorezmi, Ferghani, Javhari, Marvazi, Ulughbek; philosophers, lawyers and theologians Farabi, Bukhari, At-Termizi, Marghilani, Nasafi; encyclopedists Beruni, Ibn Sina; linguists and poets Kashghari, Yusuf Khos Khajib, Zamakhshari, Alisher Navoi; and historians Babur, Abul Ghazi Bahodirkhon and Ogahi.

The scientists of Uzbekistan continue in the line of their great ancestors. They have absorbed the best traditions and made a deep study of their historical heritage. They are marked by a thirst for knowledge, and an ambition to be part of the rising tide of advanced scientific thought. They already comprehensively contribute to the social and economic development of our Republic, they strengthen its innovative potential, and they have begun to investigate new, unknown areas of science.

In this sphere of endeavor, Uzbekistan has much to put into action. We must bring to reality innovative models of development founded on the effective and expanded use of scientific and technical possibilities; we must widely implement the modern world's achievements in the fundamental and applied sciences; we must increase the number of highly qualified scientists and technologists. These are the main requisites for a reliable basis for the country's breakthrough to the ranks of the economically and industrially developed countries of the world.

Today Uzbekistan is an important scientific center in Central Asia, possessing a highly-developed and materially well-equipped research foundation, a large scientific fund, and highly-qualified research scientists, whose research papers have been recognized by the world's scientific establishment both in theory and in practice.

Our scientific research base consists of: 362 research institutes that belong to the universities; the Academy of Sciences; 101 line-research institutes; 55 scientific research subunits at the universities; 65 organizations that design projects and propose constructions; 32 scientific production associations and experimenting enterprises; 30 informational computing centers. The heart of our scientific capacity is the Academy of Sciences, which is the leading scientific and experimental center in the region, and which was established over 60 years ago. Such scientific centers as the Institute of Nuclear Physics, the Scientific–Production Association 'Solar Physics', the Scientific–Production Association 'Biologist', and the aggregate of high mountain astronomical observatories located on Maidanak Mountain all carry out their research within the structural design of the Academy of Sciences.

About 46,000 people including 2,800 of DSc status and approximately 16,100 of PhD status carry out scientific research. For the first time in the history of the country a Supreme Commission of Certification has been established. Its function is to train young scientists. Thus the training of high-level experts in 20 branches of science is ensured. At present, scientists in the Republic are conducting research in a variety of fundamental and applied branches:

1. *In mathematics: theory of probability; mathematical modelling of natural and social processes; information and computer engineering*

The achievements of Uzbek mathematicians in the theory of probability, mathematical statistics, the theory of differential equations, mathematical physics and functional analysis are well known far beyond the boundaries of the Republic.

The foundations of the Uzbek school of astronomy were laid down by Beruni, Ulughbek and Giyasuddin Jamshid. The work of Uzbek scientists in astronomy and in the study of the movements of celestial bodies has been known from the remote past. They designed for the first time in the history of mankind the most exact map of the starry sky. The basic astronomical net has been set up in the Republic to study the climate of this area. Jointly with experts from the USA, Italy and Japan, Uzbek scientists work in the Kitab International Latitude Station, named after Ulughbek, which was built in 1930. They actively participate in international activities to study the movement of the poles on the surface of the Earth.

2. *The regularities of geological processes*

This will bring us knowledge of the formation of our mineral and raw resources (for industrial utilization), as well as knowledge of tectonics, geophysics, seismology and other Earth Sciences.

The work of Uzbek scientists in the aggregate study of geology, geophysics, the geochemical properties of the Earth's crust, ore formation and the genetics of metal and oil formation fuelled the creation of a powerful minerals and raw materials research and development base in Uzbekistan. Our geologists directly participated in the discovery, investigation and development of many big deposits of minerals in the territory of the Republic and in the whole of the Central Asian region.

As is well known, Uzbekistan is located in a seismically active zone. It has over many centuries experienced the grave consequences of natural cataclysms. That is why theoretical and applied research in seismology and into earthquake-proof constructions is considered to be very important. Uzbekistan's scientists have investigated the geological causes and conditions relating to earthquake origins, and they have developed hydro-seismological methods of forecasting earthquakes, which are used to predict the probability of their occurring. The seismic regions were determined and mapped. This made it possible to construct earthquake-proof industrial and residential buildings. The seismo-dynamic theory of underground constructions – a network of communication systems (transport and other) – is now well established.

3. *Molecular genetics; gene and cell engineering; biotechnology*

These disciplines serve as the basis for providing scientific and technical progress in agriculture, the microbiology industry and environmental protection.

Substantial scientific schools in the spheres of organic and non-organic chemistry, the chemistry of plant substances, biology, genetics and biotechnology have been founded. They have developed both the theoretical basis for and the production technology of new types of highly effective and ecologically clean fertilizers, less toxic defoliants, new medicines, plant-growth stimulators and the means of plant-protection. Also of interest for practical application are: the creation of natural and synthetic bio-regulators for medicine, agriculture, pharmacology and the food industry; the growth of stevy (a plant substitute for sugar); the creation of an ecologically safe technology to produce and process compositional polymer materials, including kaprolactam polymers; the production of high-quality cotton cellulose and acetate thread. Special mention should be made of the achievements of Uzbek selectionists who conduct research into cotton genetics, the physiological and biochemical problems of cotton biology, and the development of selection methods of new, high-quality, disease-proof sorts of cotton. Over recent years, more than 30 types of cotton have been developed for long-term cultivation.

4. *The physical and chemical properties of matter*

Fundamental research in the physics of the nucleus and the elementary particles, and in radiation physics, has been especially well developed in the Republic. A school of relativistic nuclear physics is well-established. It serves as the theoretical basis for research into nuclear energy and applied nuclear physics. Uzbekistan has world-recognized priorities in radiation research. The Republic is a leading center for the production of radioactive isotopes, as well as pharmaceutical radio-materials.

A school of high energy physics has been established. A solid scientific base has been set up in the foundation of this school to obtain especially pure, highly fireproof materials, and to create a new technology for the production of high-temperature materials that have a high wear-out stability, fire resistance and corrosion resistance, and a capability of being substituted for expensive construction materials.

A great deal of work is being carried out on the creation of non-traditional types of energy, most particularly and importantly the complex and effective transformation and utilization of solar energy.

5. *World and Motherland-history; our cultural and spiritual heritage; the historical and current development of Uzbek language, literature and folklore*

Work in the social sciences and the humanities, especially that of historians, archaeologists, ethnographers, linguists and literary critics, has contributed much to the development of the intellectual potential of the Republic, and to the expansion of its international cultural links. Work connected with research in ethnogenesis, with the recreation of the objective history of the Uzbek nation, and with the study of its traditions, way of life and culture is of exceptional interest and importance.

The development of our own intellectual, scientific and technical potential, which we treat as a vital factor in the stable and solid progress of our country, is directly connected with the further expansion of our scientific, technical and cultural links with the best research centers of the world.

Taking into account the specific peculiarities of the demographic situation in Uzbekistan, the development of our human potential needs a corresponding level of the development of our social infrastructure, particularly in the areas of health and the social services.
The Republic has a developed system of medical and social services that provides wide access to various kinds of general medical and highly specialized medical services. There are over 1,300 hospitals, and more than 3,000 outpatient clinics; a wide net of rural medical centers has been created. More than 76,000 doctors in all branches of medicine provide qualified medical help; on average one doctor looks after 298 people. This index is better than in many developing countries of the world. Thus, if comparison is made with Turkey, the United Arab Emirates and Korea, we see that the qualified medical service in Uzbekistan is 3–4 times higher; in comparison with Malaysia, India and Pakistan it is 6–8 times higher.

The public utilities services provided to the population is well developed. Primarily, they are electricity, mains water and natural gas supply. Special programs are being developed and successfully implemented to supply the rural population with drinking water and gas. The result of this is that 73 per cent of the housing stock of the Republic is provided with mains water supply and 64 per cent with natural gas; all the residential areas are supplied with electricity.

At the same time, in order further to improve living conditions, especially in ecologically complex regions close to the Aral Sea, much attention is now being paid to improving the general epidemiological situation: to decreasing the level of infectious diseases and deaths among children, and to improve the supply of good quality drinking water. To this end, not only are substantial funds and services from the government being delivered to these regions, but also the funds and services of many international economic and humanitarian organizations.

The great advantage of Uzbekistan, from the point of view of its international contacts, is that we have developed energy, communication and water systems, and a unified network of roads and railroads. It is an inescapable fact that the prospects for economic development in any country are defined by the availability of its own energy base. Uzbekistan has a powerful energy system, which is part of the unified energy system of Central

Asia. Geographically Uzbekistan is located in the center of the region, and it generates half the power of the energy system of all power stations of the unified energy system of Central Asia. Uzbekistan's energy system is the main link in the indivisible chain of the production and transmission of electric power into the region.

At the core of the Uzbek energy system stand the big thermo-electric power stations such as Syrdarya-Tashkent, Novo-Angren and Navoi; and the 19 other hydro-electric power stations, the Charvak plant being the biggest among them. At present a special program of the construction of small hydro-electric plants is being developed in order to use the hydro-electric potential of rivers, reservoirs and canals for the needs of energy and irrigation, and to improve the electricity supply in rural areas. The Uzbek energy system fully meets the Republic's needs for electric power and is able to export it to neighboring states. The current capacity of existing electric power stations can provide enough electric power for all investment projects being implemented in Uzbekistan in the foresee-able future without the construction of new generating capacity. Nevertheless, construction of the Novo-Angren thermo-electric power station and the Mubarek thermo-electric power station is scheduled for completion by 2000. Also scheduled is the putting into operation of the first energy bloc of the Talimarjan electric power station.

Uzbekistan has a developed gas pipeline system with nine main gas pipelines, the total length of which is 12,000 kilometers. These lines provide an exit into the unified system of gas of the CIS. This makes it possible to supply large amounts of gas not only to the countries of Central Asia and the CIS, but also to the countries of Europe. The construction in future of interstate main gas pipelines – Turkmenistan-Uzbekistan-Kazakhstan-China and also Uzbeki-stan-Afghanistan-Pakistan – which are today under detailed study, will enable the export potential of the oil-gas sector of the Republic to increase by more than eight times.

Another important factor in Uzbekistan's geostrategic location is the developed system of transport communication. Today our transport system satisfies all our domestic transportation needs. We have the highest density of road and railroad networks in

Central Asia. The length of railroads is over 6,700 kilometers and many of these railroads are supplied with electric power. Over 80 per cent of all roads have hard covering. The dominant roads of the Republic are roads of international and state significance, which have an improved type of hard covering. The existing network of rail and road transport communications not only safely connects our most distant regions to the most populated areas of the Republic and provides an exit into international transport systems, but also provides a wide access to the main sources of the natural and raw-mineral resources of our rich region.

Uzbekistan is advantageously situated in regard to the development of international air communications. Being located half-way between Europe and Eastern Asia, the Republic serves as a highly effective international transport junction, providing air transit transportation of passengers and cargo. The Uzbek National Airline 'Uzbekiston Havo Yullari' is a member of ICAO and has within its structure, besides Tashkent airport, 12 more regional airports, three of which are fit to receive airliners of international class. The reconstruction of airports in the cities of Tashkent, Samarkand, Bukhara, Urgench, Namangan and Termez is being implemented with the help of foreign capital and foreign experts. A new airport is under construction in the heart of our main 'store-cupboard' of mineral resources, Uchquduk. At present direct air links connect Uzbekistan with the main cities in many countries of the world: e.g. New York, London, Frankfurt, Athens, Tel-Aviv, Bangkok, Seoul, New Delhi.

After the Republic gained its independence much attention was paid to international systems of transport in order to create the shortest and most reliable roads that would provide access to our neighboring states and to the world's oceans. This problem is conditioned by the geographical location of the Republic. For several decades, our economic contacts with foreign countries were mainly through railroads, with cargo transported via the ports of the former Soviet Union on the shores of the Black, Baltic, Japanese and Northern Seas. It has to be said that such transportation was over-expensive, and that transport communications to the South were not developed.

After the collapse of the USSR, the problem of external communications for Uzbekistan became even more acute because, in order to have an exit to sea ports, we have to cross the territories of several countries. We are located very far from sea ports and the shortest route is 3,000 kilometers – the greatest distance in this respect in the whole world. Naturally, this limits the Republic's possibilities for developing wide economic links and makes us dependent for transport on the countries through which our goods must pass. Owing to ever-growing and highly inflated tariffs, this makes our goods uncompetitive.

World experience testifies, and Uzbekistan is another proof of it, that the country that has no direct access to the sea significantly suffers in export economic terms. That is why we are persisting in finding alternative ways of solving the problem of how to provide our exports with an effective and economic transport system, and of how to gain access to the world's oceans. For this purpose Uzbekistan participates in the UN program 'expansion of trade through the development of co-operation in transit transportation'. Within this program the Central Asian countries are jointly developing commercial and tourist transport corridors, by means of which access to sea ports will be provided and the recreation of the ancient commercial main route, the Great Silk Road, will be stimulated.

The Intergovernmental Treaty has already been signed between the Republics of Central Asia and the countries of the Economic Co-operation Organization (ECO) and the construction is under way of the Tejen-Serakhs-Mashhad railroad, which is a constituent part of the trans-Asian main route that connects Peking to Istanbul. After completion by 2000 the cargo flows in both directions are expected to amount to 6–8 million tons, and in future this figure will double. The opening of this transport corridor will give added impulse to the increase of trade contacts between Uzbekistan and the East – with the countries of the Asian Pacific region – and also the West – with Turkey and the rest of Europe; in both directions the length of the route will be cut by half, in comparison with the present system.

In the widening and strengthening of the narrow, weak joints in our land's communication and transport capacities, of great importance is the TRESEKA project, with technical assistance provided by the European Union, which is part of the TACIS program that is setting up the transcaucasian main line that will pass through the territories of Central Asian countries, through Azerbaijan and Georgia, to the ports of the Black Sea. We are also eager to participate in the construction or reconstruction of the Andijan-Osh-Irkashtam-Kashgar road which opens us up to China and Pakistan and also the Bukhara-Serahs-Mashhad-Teheran and Termez-Herat-Kandagar-Karachi roads, which will also make it possible to reach the Indian Ocean. This transport corridor is three times shorter than the route to the ECO countries.

After the completion of construction and fortification work on these transcontinental main lines, conditions will be favorable for improving the export capacities of Uzbekistan and the other Central Asian countries by expanding cargo and passenger transit transportation from the Asian Pacific region, India and China to the countries of the Middle East, Turkey and Europe. Along these routes, which coincide with the direction of the Great Silk Road, it is possible to establish regular cultural, tourist and business contacts with many countries of the world. This will, essentially, open for the countries of the CIS and Central Asia the 'southern road' to world markets and for the countries of South Asia, South-East Asia and the Middle East the 'northern road' to Central Asian markets.

In order to create favorable conditions for developing and strengthening international transport and economic contacts Uzbekistan is today implementing a number of organizational and legal measures.

1. We understand very well that investment in transport communications is an expensive and low-profit business. Nevertheless, Uzbekistan at its own expense has begun the construction of two large and strategically important main railroad lines – Navoi-Uchquduq-Sultanuizdag-Nukus, which is 342 kilometers and Guzar-Boisun-Qumqurgan, 223 kilometers – as well as the reconstruction of the Angren-Kokand road. The use of these lines and roads will not only provide access to our richest deposits

of natural minerals and reduce the cost of transportation inside the Republic, but will also provide an exit-access to sea ports to international transport communications.

2. The Republic is persisting in bringing our legislation that regulates transport relations up to international standards. Thus, in the sphere of automobile transportation, the Customs Convention on International Cargo Transportation, the Convention on Traffic Signs and Signals, and the Convention on Traffic Movement were ratified.

In the sphere of civil aviation, the Convention on the illegal seizure of aircraft, the Convention on crimes and other acts committed on board aircraft, the Convention on the unification of rules concerning international air transportation were also ratified. The Government of Uzbekistan has also ratified 13 more protocols associated with the changes in the Convention on International Civil Aviation.

Work is being carried out to join, in the near future, 17 more conventions and agreements on different issues connected with the organization of international transportation.

3. Favorable conditions are being created for setting up joint ventures with foreign partners in the spheres of transport services and systems of communication. Among ventures already operational in international air transportation are those with Asia Rianta (jointly with the Irish company Air Rianta International and Shannon airport), Askon (jointly with the American corporation Concord); AIRO ABDA (jointly with the Malaysian company, Abdy Freight), Interservice Cargo (jointly with the United Arab Emirates).

Similar ventures are in train in the automobile sphere within the structure of the International Auto-transportation of Uzbekistan (ASMAP), which promotes the implementation of an effective transport policy in the sphere of international automobile transportation and protects our national interests in regard to such transportation.

4. The Republic jointly with leading foreign companies such as Motorolla (USA), Siemens, Alcatel (Germany) and Daewoo

(South Korea), is carrying out the construction of modern tele-communication networks and computer systems.

The creation and development of our social and industrial infra-structure, as outlined above, with the substantial support of the state is helping to improve the investment climate in the Republic, to reduce the expenditure of foreign investors in the creation of joint produc-tions, and significantly to reduce the time of the putting into operation of new capacities and enterprises (which demonstrably increases the return of invested capital).

Chapter Fifteen

Guarantees for large-scale transformation and co-operation

The building of an open democratic state and of a market economy is being carried out in Uzbekistan on an internationally recognized constitutional basis that provides strong legislative guarantees and conditions for the reforming of the economy and its integration with the world economic community.

The First Constitution and the entire code of basic laws adopted in the Republic serve as a solid legal guarantee for democratization in all spheres of life, for the irreversibility of our society's renovation processes, and for co-operation with the many countries of the world that regard Uzbekistan as a reliable current or prospective partner.

We have drawn a simple conclusion: the irreversibility and sustainability of our advancement to a democratic society and a market economy depend directly on its sound legal basis. Only with a strong legal foundation will it be possible to deconstruct the old, obsolete system and build a new society with a highly developed and efficient market economy. *The supremacy of the law is a leading principle in our model of reform and it serves as one of the main criteria of our new law-governed state.* Our great ancestor Amir Timur ordered the inscription in gold letters of this wise saying: 'Where the law reigns, there is the freedom.' Examining our legislative activity during the 1990s, we can distinguish the following principal blocks of the legal acts adopted in the country:

1. Laws directed at strengthening our state system and improving our state bodies. They embrace a system of laws targeted at securing the protection of the national interest, at strengthening our defense capability and security, and at forming bodies concerned with state authority and administration. These latter bodies, guided by the principle of the separation of powers, are the basic elements in the implementation of reforms and the creation of a law-governed state and a civil society. They are at the people's service, ensuring their rights and freedoms.
2. Laws aimed at creating a legal basis for the implementation of economic reforms; laws targeted at securing the social protection of citizens, forming a class of proprietors, creating conditions for the equitable development of all forms of property and entrepreneurship, and upgrading financial, banking and tax policies.
3. Laws that create a legal foundation for the liberalization and democratization of our political system, and for the implementation of an effective mechanism to protect human rights and freedoms. These laws have established a legal basis for the wider participation of citizens in the management of their society, and for the free and improved activity of the press and mass media.
4. Laws that identify Uzbekistan as an entity within international law, regulate the external political and economic relations of the Republic, and create solid legal guarantees for broad and active international collaboration.

We are aware that none of these blocks of laws is able to perform independently, without an interrelationship with the other blocks of laws. Only through interacting, complementing and enriching each other will they create a sufficiently solid basis for the transformation and reform of society. For instance, when we speak about a legal basis that guarantees the irreversibility of market reforms we cannot limit ourselves to only one block of laws. The entire set of laws dealing with all aspects of life in society and, above all, the Constitution itself, lay down the legal foundation for market transformations.

I should stress that one of the key principles of the legal development of the Republic is the primacy of international law over domestic legislation. This is shown not only in the continued unification of our legislation, in its approximation to universally recognized international standards and regulations, but also in the Republic's undertakings to assume all the obligations that will guarantee the execution of international laws.

Solid constitutional bases have been laid down for the formation, promotion and upgrading of social and political relations, the economic freedom of citizens, free entrepreneurship and the repudiation of the old command-administrative management system. The Constitution ensures that it is a law-governed state that protects the economic foundation of our society, i.e. *a multi-structured market economy and the private property of its citizens.*

For the first time in the last 75 years legislation now ensures that private property, along with other forms of property, is inviolable and protected by the state. Our Basic Law serves as a powerful barrier against any monopolistic right of the state to interfere in the economic sphere, provides for free economic activity, guarantees the rights and inherent legal interests of the private entrepreneur, creates conditions for open and fair competition, and generally opens up the wide road to the free and fair market.

The constitutional right to private property granted to the citizen strengthens his feeling of self-respect, his independence from another's will, and his initiatives and creative roles in the renovation and development of our society. The Constitution declares: 'The economy of Uzbekistan, evolving towards market relations, is based on various forms of ownership. The state shall guarantee freedom of economic activity, entrepreneurship and labor with due regard for the priority of consumers' rights, and for equality of and legal protection of all forms of ownership.'

The stability of a state's legal system is a major guarantee for economic development and for the protection of invested capital. In contrast with a number of other post-Soviet countries, which over a short period of time adopted more than one constitution, here over Uzbekistan we have firmly adhered to the principle of legal stability. Our whole system of legislative activity is focused on the creation of new laws and on the improvement of those already in force, taking us along the path of reform and taking into account changing conditions. Alongside this, there are reliable guarantees against changes in our legislation. For instance, if changes in legislation worsen an investment's conditions, then the previous legal norms that were in force at the time of the investment continue to be applicable to foreign investors for 10 years.

Based on the constitutional provisions that regulate our foreign policy principles, the laws 'On the Basic Principles of our External Political Activity', 'On Foreign Investments and Guarantees for the Activity of Foreign Investors', 'On External Economic Activity' have been adopted, along with a series of other regulatory acts that enable us to promote external economic activity, to create a favorable climate for foreign investors and to expand trading links with foreign businessmen. We have created a legal and organizational environment for the integration of our society with world civilization and for investment in our economy. Uzbekistan conducts a so-called 'open door' policy, granting to foreign investors reliable legal guarantees and broad economic opportunities for business activity. An environment highly favorable to foreign investors has been established and is constantly being improved. Procedures for creating manufacturing enterprises with foreign assets have been simplified to the maximum.

The regulatory acts adopted in the Republic have created a comprehensive system of tax benefits and incentives, guarantees against political and commercial risks, as well as favorable conditions for the active participation of foreign companies in the markets of Uzbekistan. Here are four basic guarantees granted to foreign investors by current legislation:

1. Foreign investments in the Republic of Uzbekistan shall not be subject to nationalization and requisition.
2. Foreign investors are guaranteed profits and other assets in foreign currency obtained as a result of legal economic activity, without any restrictions, as well as the unconditional conversion of profits obtained as a result of importing raw materials, components and modern technologies.
3. The freedom to purchase property that the state has privatized, including real estate, is guaranteed to foreign persons. Foreign investors are entitled to ownership rights, including the ownership

of trading and services units, houses with plots of land, and other land and natural resources.

4. Enterprises with foreign investments are entitled to export without licence products of their own manufacture and to import commodities for their own production purposes, as well as to import duty-free property as joint venture charter fund contributions.

Apart from these guarantees, current legislation grants foreign investors a broad range of tax incentives.

- They are exempt from income tax for a term of seven years if they participate in those project investments that are part of the state investment program.
- Part of the income of enterprises with foreign investment that is directed at production expansion and technological re-equipment is also tax exempt.
- Assets of joint ventures directed to refinance and to the extinguishment of loans obtained for investment are exempt from taxation.
- Differential rates of income tax for industrial enterprises with foreign capital have been introduced. These stipulate the reduction of tax rates according to the share in the joint venture charter fund contributions.
- Joint ventures with foreign capital share of more than 30 per cent specializing in the production and processing of agricultural products, consumer goods and building materials, medical equipment, machinery and equipment for agriculture, light and food industry, processing of recycled materials and communal waste are exempt from income tax for two years following their registration.
- Property delivered into the Republic for personal needs, and a foreign partner's property contribution to the authorized capital of enterprises with foreign investment, are exempt from custom duties, as well as the property of foreigners with a direct investment in Uzbekistan's economy amounting in total to more than US$50 million.

173

This is an incomplete list of privileges which are now in force for enterprises with foreign investments. Apart from this, enterprises with foreign assets share some other tax privileges that are granted to all enterprises of the Republic.

In order to render assistance to foreign investors in Uzbekistan a network of specialized organizations and agencies has been established: Foreign Investments Agency, Chamber of Commodity Producers and Entrepreneurs, National Company of Export-Import Insurance, Uzbekinvest. In collaboration with AIG (USA), a joint insurance company against political risks, Uzbekinvest International, has been created, with its headquarters in London. A leasing company has been established, the founders of which are the International Financial Corporation, European Bank for Reconstruction and Development, Malaysian Bank Berhad (Malaysia) and our local National Bank for External Economic Activity.

A reliable insurance protection of foreign investment in the Republic is provided, at lower insurance rates than the international average. In cases of non-payment foreign creditors who have invested their capital in the Republic have the opportunity to present their claims on the insurance case with a term of 30 days, although international practice has established a term of 180 days.

These guarantees, privileges and incentives that exist for foreign investors in the Republic testify that Uzbekistan is an advantageous country in which to invest assets.

We attach great importance not only to the radical transformation of the legislative system, but also to the implementation of agreed actions of the legislative and executive branches of the government in the realization of existing laws and other regulatory acts. We regard it as essential to apply existing laws to everyday life.

Law, in contrast with the arbitrary dictates of the former administrative-command system, is for us the universal tool of social management, a rule for each agency's performance, for every citizen's behavior. In sum, during these years of independence a broad legal space has been created in the Republic that is based on internationally recognized legal principles and standards that proceed from the priority of human rights and freedoms and serve as a guarantee for the irreversibility of reforms, progress and mutually beneficial co-operation.

World experience, and our own experience, accumulated in recent years, testify that *the major condition for our successful effecting of large-scale transformations in the economic, political and cultural spheres, for the radical transformation of our social relations, and for international recognition and active international co-operation is the ensurance of social and political stability, civil peace and inter-ethnic harmony.* It cannot be said too strongly that the preservation of social and political stability, particularly during the most difficult transition period, is the basis for the implementation of a reliable state policy for a long-term period. This, in its turn, is the basic condition for the consolidation of our state system, the strengthening of our international relations, and the wide involvement of foreign investment in our reforming economy.

It is well known that foreign investors and investments will only come to a country where legal backing for their activities are provided, where real conditions for their stable activities exist, where social and political stability exist, where political risks are reduced to a minimum, and where centers of inter-ethnic and civil disagreement are absent. A fine legislative basis for the reform of the economy and for interested foreign investors may be created, and progressive laws may be adopted, but if a society lacks stability, if there are no guarantees against political shocks, civil wars and regional conflicts, then it becomes irrelevant to speak about the application of existing laws, or about the investment flows that are necessary for the structural changes in the reforming of our economy.

It is the stability in our society and the predictability of our state policy that constitute the basis for the implementation of large-scale radical transformations, and of realistic, attractive investment activities. That is why two closely interrelated problems — successful reform and sustainable development on the one hand, and the preservation of social and political stability on the other hand — *constitute the core of the policy of the Republic.*

It is precisely the preservation of social and political stability that is the distinctive feature of Uzbekistan as an independent state. Uzbekistan was one of the first post-Soviet countries to have the sorrowful experience of terrible events that lead to the destabilization of the social and political situation in any society: destructive and endless debates and mass-meetings, as well as political, national and religious extremism.

Uzbekistan started implementing its reforms when its initial social and political possibilities were much worse in comparison with the majority of the Republics of the former USSR. These conditions were: a 'demographic explosion' threat, limited availability of suitable land for normal life, a hypertrophically developed one-sided economy, and the totalitarian supression of the national self-identification of the Uzbek nation – all of which generated internal destabilization and created a situation of serious social tension in our society.

Having witnessed the tragic events in Ferghana, Osh, and Buka, the people of Uzbekistan were one of the first to realize the catastrophe to which religious and interethnic rivalry may lead. The people became aware that social and political confrontation, nihilism, extremist rejection of all that was positive in our heritage and pressure exerted by rallies and meetings could only aggravate the acute problems that we had inherited from the previous regime. The people became aware of the danger of the pseudo-patriots' demagogy, of political intriguers, dilettantes, careerists and irresponsible groups of different kinds who, for the sake of reaching power, were ready to bring the country to a national catastrophe.

The people of Uzbekistan saw clearly what kind of danger it was, and saw that if it was not stopped it was capable of blowing up our entire society, of being a catalyst of irreversible processes of destabilization and disintegration, of being a barrier to the pace of the renovation, reform, rebirth and consolidation of the Republic as an independent and sovereign state.

The bitter experience of the recent past convinces us again and again that the formation of an open democratic and legal state can be carried out only under two conditions: if the people will accept (a) all the significance of social and political stability and (b) that law and order in the country should be supported, with every citizen participating in the transformation that is taking place in their society.

The multi-ethnic people of the Republic have accepted the consolidation idea: that Uzbekistan is a state with a great future.

They have supported the course of reform and this has become the foundation for both social harmony and the strategy for the development of their state and their society. Now, after several years of independence and sovereignty as a Republic, it is difficult to overestimate the role and significance of the nationwide ideas and tasks that must be brought into play to consolidate our society. In the most difficult period of the consolidation of our new national state system we have managed to erect a reliable barrier against various destabilizing factors and threats that could split society according to political, religious and ethnic groupings.

To sum up, it is possible to draw the conclusion that social and political stability has been achieved in Uzbekistan as a result of:

1. The deep understanding in our society that the disastrous consequences of inter-ethnic contradictions and civil confrontations are based on narrow group interests – the most powerful factor in the disintegration and destabilization of society.
2. The design and implementation of (a) a well-thought-out program of radical reforms endorsed by the people, and (b) strong measures of state for the social protection of the people, which are the basis for a social consensus on the major priorities and objectives of the development of society.
3. The creation and effective functioning of the new system of state authority and management bodies that are based on the principles of the democratic separation of powers; the expansion of local government and self-government; and the formation of a broad legal pattern for the active, and, what is more important, the constructive activity of different political and social movements and non-governmental organizations, in order to preserve and consolidate the rule of law.

We are perfectly aware that, without providing such conditions, there is no possibility of our carrying through our economic reforms to introduce a market economy, to change our forms of property, and, indeed, to renovate our society. *We bear in mind that it is stability in our society that constitutes our basic wealth, and the guarantor for our further successful development.* It follows that only when such stability has been achieved can social and political parties and movements have the opportunity widely and openly to discuss issues concerning social development, to reach their goals, to realize their potential, to take part in the formation of our democratic state and our institutions of social authority.

It must finally be emphasized once again that social and political stability is the major basis and condition for the dynamic and consistent development of our society, and for its integration into the world system. It is especially important that we maintain stability during this most complicated period when social and economic contradictions are aggravated by the transitional character of many social transformations. Thus we should understand stability as a concept with the broadest meaning, since social and political stability, and national and civil harmony, are the basis and guarantee for the renovation and reform of our society, and for our goal of sustainable development.

Chapter Sixteen

Integration with the world community

In the short period of Uzbekistan's independent development, much work has been done to consolidate the Republic as a sovereign state. Today 165 states officially recognize Uzbekistan. Diplomatic relations have been established with more than 120 states, and 35 states have opened embassies in Tashkent.

Uzbekistan is a fully fledged member of prestigious and influential international organizations, is building up friendly relations with dozens of countries on every continent, and co-operates closely with major banking and financial institutions and non-governmental organizations. Some 88 foreign associations have accreditation in the Republic, and 24 governmental and 13 non-governmental organizations carry on their work here. In recent years the Republic has put its signature to many important international Conventions.

In regard to its external political and economic links Uzbekistan is committed to the following main principles, worked out in the first years of independence:

1. The supremacy of Uzbekistan's interests within the overall consideration of mutual interests;
2. Equity and mutual benefit, and non-interference in the internal affairs of other states;
3. An openness to co-operation irrespective of ideological conceptions, and a commitment to universal values, peace and security;

4. The primacy of the standards of international law with regard to domestic law;

5. The promotion of external relations through both bilateral and multilateral agreements.

We consider the successful development of links in various fields of international relations as a guarantee for security and stability. Uzbekistan is open to the world. But we also feel that the world shows great interest in Uzbekistan. This is the best guarantee for Uzbekistan's sustainable development. In this we see proof that Uzbekistan is becoming more and more attractive from the point of view both of investment and of ensuring stability in the region, which is an integral component of overall global security.

While embarking on our strategic task of building up a modern democratic state that is integrated with the world community, we are aware that the international community itself is becoming multi-dimensional. The end of the twentieth century is marked by changes that have geopolitical scope and significance. These are unprecedented changes that require not only deep evaluation but also in many cases a revision of the traditional attitudes and mechanisms of relations between countries. Many postulates, principles and ideas on which the international relations of the 'cold war' period were based today demand radical revision. The world is becoming an integral and interrelated system in which there is no place for autarchy and isolation. This makes it necessary to work out new approaches to international relations and interactions with international entities.

The twenty-first century is likely to be the century of the globalization of international relations. Therefore this process of integration – the growing participation of sovereign states in international organizations – should be regarded not only as a historical necessity but also as a powerful way of providing sustainability and stability both in separate regions and over the entire planet.

The question is not whether to take part or not in international integration processes. For Uzbekistan, a new independent state, it is of decisive importance that we should observe the above-mentioned principles of foreign policy, based on reasonable expediency and on the long-term interests of the state, the society and the individual.

Independence for us is not a simple awareness of our freedom, but first of all it is the right to build up our lives and future with our own hands according to our will and national interests. So it is quite natural that there should be no integration dictated or imposed from outside, if it infringes the freedom, independence and territorial integrity of our country or is tied up with certain ideological obligations.

When talking about integration we proceed from the fact that there are various mechanisms that govern mutual interests and types of integration. These mechanisms are conditioned by the different initial levels of the countries seeking partnership and co-operation. Uzbekistan participates in integrational processes on various levels, global and regional, but it retains a very important principle: *rapprochement with one state does not imply moving away from another.* Strengthening a partnership with one country should not take place at the expense of weakening a partnership with another. So the integration of Uzbekistan into the world community is a multi-vectoral process.

We subscribe to the idea that integration with the world community can only happen provided a state holds to the modern concepts of democracy and a market economy. It is possible to modernize a country only if it is integrated into the world community, that is if it has its own proper place in the international division of labor, and actively participates in regional and global security systems.

The deeper and wider the relations of Uzbekistan with various international entities, the less will be uncertainty, estrangement, problems, unsolved issues and elements of unpredictibility in our relations with them. This is a necessary condition for the elimination of threats to our security and for the provision of sustainable development. We believe that the degree of a state's security directly depends on how it participates in integration processes. The formula in this case is absolutely clear: the threat to a state's security is in inverse proportion to its level of integration.

When we speak about integration with the world community, we mean primarily our membership of the United Nations Organisation, which we joined on March 2nd, 1992. We regard our participation in this organization as an opportunity to draw world attention to the acute problems of ensuring security, peace and harmony in the Central

Asian region. Today, among the various international organizations concerned with the problem of global security, only the UN has at its disposal a complete set of means ranging from preventive diplomacy to peacemaking operations to secure and maintain it.

On Uzbekistan's initiative an international meeting-seminar on the issues of security and co-operation in Central Asia was successfully held under the aegis of the UN in 1995 in Tashkent. Diplomatic and government representatives from 20 international organizations and over 30 countries took part in the meeting, including the USA, Germany, France, Great Britain, Russia, Japan, China, India, Pakistan and Iran.

Our relations with the UN are not exclusively based on a desire to receive the support of the international community, although this is very important for us today, but quite as much on a desire to render our all-round assistance with the successful implementation of UN programs and to help to fill its activities with new contents. The changing geopolitical situation in the world requires that the organization and activities of the UN in the new millennium be updated. Some countries have emerged which, owing to their growing power and influence on world politics, might well become permanent members of the Security Council. Further, not just the structure of the UN, but also its functioning, its procedures, and the implementation of its actions still have the traces of the past struggles between the great powers for spheres of influence. This is part of the reason why UN peacemaking operations and attempts at conflict settlement are not always successful. That is why Uzbekistan will actively support the upgrading of the structure and performance of this organization.

It is necessary to point out that the potential of integration through the United Nations is huge. The components of this potential are the specialized agencies with which Uzbekistan is today in fruitful co-operation. Integration with the world community through the UN is precisely for us co-operation with such UN agencies as UNESCO, World Health Organization, International Labour Organization, UNCTAD and UNICEF.

Such international financial and economic organizations as the International Monetary Fund, World Bank, International Financial Corporation, European Bank for Reconstruction and Development and others render great assistance in the implementation of our economic reforms, supporting Uzbekistan to integrate with the world community. We attach great importance to our country's participation in the World Economic Forum held annually in Davos. For one thing, we need to participate in the Forum in order to present Uzbekistan and its potential to attract foreign investments.

Another component in the integration processes with the world community is the expansion of our relationships with various regional associations. We are fruitfully co-operating with such regional and international organizations as the EU, OSCE, NATO, ECO, OIC and The Non-Aligned Movement.

The European Union occupies a special place in this list. The year of 1996 was marked by several important events in the development of the relationship between the EU and Uzbekistan.

In February the Council of the EU at ministerial level decided to start negotiations with Uzbekistan to conclude an Agreement on Partnership and Co-operation, and in July it was signed in Florence. Uzbekistan is the second state, after Russia, in post-Soviet territory to sign such an Agreement.

The European orientation in Uzbekistan's foreign policy has been considerably expanded: it comprises co-operation both with individual European countries and with the EU itself.

We consider our partnership and co-operation with the EU as one more way of ensuring the security and development of Uzbekistan, because this kind of partnership involves not just the economic, cultural and scientific spheres, but also the military sphere. This Agreement opens up a new stage of co-operation, creates a legal basis for the interrelationship between Uzbekistan, the EU and individual European member-states, presents wide opportunities for economic, scientific, technical and cultural links, and lays down an institutional basis for regular political dialogue.

The signed Agreement not only testifies to the mutual desire to create the foundation for an active partnership. It is testimony that a democratic society is being successfully built in Uzbekistan, and that our nations are linked by such common values as respect for human rights, civic freedoms and the law-governed state.

I would like to emphasise the fruitful co-operation that exists with the Organization on Security and Co-operation in Europe (OSCE). The level of co-operation is expressed through measures carried out jointly with the OSCE, OSCE officials' visits to Uzbekistan and the flourishing of the OSCE's Regional Office for Central Asia, which has been opened in Tashkent.

Our participation in the Lisbon summit of December 1996 was a major event in the development of relations between Uzbekistan and the OSCE. Within the framework of this forum Uzbekistan was given the right and opportunity to present its own view of the security problem. Our appeal for more active efforts by the OSCE in Central Asia received support and understanding and was ratified in the Lisbon Declaration. In fact, that was the time when the OSCE in its documents expressed its intention to maintain stability and prevent confrontation in this region.

In the Lisbon discussions about the universal security model on the eve of the twenty-first century, we again reiterated our full support for the fundamental principles of the indivisibility of security. It is pleasing that our proposal to put an end to illegal armament supplies to conflict zones was reflected in the final document of the Lisbon meeting. We hope that eventually this will be an integral part of the universal security model for the twenty-first century.

Apart from this, on Uzbekistan's initiative a series of larger OSCE forums were held recently in Tashkent. The international meeting-seminar arranged by the Office of Democratic Institutes and Human Rights (ODIHR) of the OSCE, 'National Institutes on Human Rights', provided an opportunity for broad dialogue with experts from 21 countries of Central Asia, Europe and America, as well as representatives of 29 international and non-governmental organizations. They discussed issues concerning the performance of ombudsmen institutes in Central and Eastern Europe, national human rights institutes, updating legislative systems, and also the role of public education and the mass media in the sphere of human rights.

On the ODIHR–OSCE initiative a seminar entitled 'The role of mass media in democratic processes' was held. An international seminar organized by the OSCE Court for Reconciliation and

Arbitration was also held. All this is real proof of close and fruitful contacts with this peace-making and human rights protection organization.

Today it is possible to speak about mutual understanding and co-operation between our country and such international organizations as NATO.

We think that NATO, which is comprised of democratic states, may become a stabilizing force not only on the European continent, but also, by strengthening its political structure and the 'Partnership for Peace' program, in the vast Eurasian region. Our participation in the 'Partnership for Peace' program we regard as strengthening our independence and sovereignty, as connecting ourselves to modern military and technical achievements, and as expanding opportunities in our military experts' training.

The visits of Secretary-General Solana and the permanent US representative in NATO Hunter to Uzbekistan demonstrated shared attitudes towards global and regional security problems. Negotiations have revealed full understanding and support of our initiatives directed at attaining peace in the region, at the regulation of confrontation in Afghanistan by political means, and at declaring the Central Asian region a nuclear-free zone. We share the point of view that regards developing Uzbekistan's potential as a stabilizing factor in the region.

The European component of Uzbekistan's integration with the world community is vitally important from the viewpoint of our national interests. Europe and the West as a whole are a source of high technology and investment, and a symbol of modern democracy and human rights. The young state of Uzbekistan has made renovation and progress its strategic objective in order to enter the twenty-first century as a modern democratic state with ensured security and stable development. We affirm the principle of 'reciprocal conditionality between security and development'. This implies, on the one hand, the provision of a stable and safe environment for investment in the economy; on the other hand, only a country that is carrying out large-scale reforms in all spheres of life is capable of ensuring such a safe environment.

Close co-operation with other international organizations, primarily from the Asian region, also helps us along the road of the intensification of stable democratic reforms. I would here like to underline especially the development and deepening of relations with the Turkic-speaking countries. It is a great satisfaction that, within the framework of already traditional summits of these countries' leaders, a destructive process of politicization, character-istic of the initial independence period, has been overcome. Today the participants focus their attention on the solution of current economic and humanitarian problems for their peoples' prosperity.

The fourth Meeting of the Heads of Turkic-speaking States was held in Tashkent in October 1996, which proved once again that the historical, ethnic, cultural and spiritual closeness of these nations serves as the basis for the relationships between the Turkic-speaking states. This closeness creates reliable guarantees for peace and security in this controversial region. During the meeting special attention was paid to the further development of bilateral and multilateral collaboration in the areas of science, culture, education, economics and transport communications. It was planned to implement a jointly-designed program, 'the restoration of the Silk Road via the promotion of educational tourism and the revival, preservation and development of the cultural heritage of the Turkic-speaking states'. This is aimed at expanding the network of tourist routes and the corresponding tourism infrastructure.

As it has been pointed out, Uzbekistan is committed to building up its external links on both a multilateral and a bilateral basis. The widening of such contacts enables us all to consider more concretely our mutual interests, to know each other more closely, and to lay down a solid foundation for long-lasting, mutually beneficial co-operation, and for stability and security.

Our bilateral contacts with the United States of America develop consistently and steadily in regard to important aspects of our relationship. The official visit of an Uzbekistan delegation to the USA in the summer of 1996 has contributed to this. During this visit meetings were held with President Clinton and other senior officials. Stemming from this, Uzbek–American political consultations take place regularly. The development and deepening of multifaceted relations with the USA, the leading world power with its huge political, economic, military, technical and intellectual resources, is today of primary significance for us. The United States makes a substantial contribution to our processes of renovation, reform and democratization in the strengthening of our independence and sovereignty. We acknowledge the increasing importance of the implementation of joint investment projects with US companies, of the establishment of long-lasting, mutually-beneficial links of partnership, and of the expansion of US capital in our markets.

In recent years our direct, bilateral relations with many European countries, including Germany, Great Britain, France, Belgium, Portugal, Austria, Greece, the Czech Republic, Slovakia and Romania have been considerably expanded and consolidated. I am pleased to report that our meetings and frank discussions with the heads of state and government of these countries have confirmed the similarity of our approaches and views on the main political issues. This opens great prospects for our close long-term co-operation, and for the expansion of trade.

With special satisfaction I would like to stress the strengthening of our relations with the countries of East and South-East Asia: Japan, South Korea, China, Vietnam, Malaysia, India and Indonesia. Recently Japan has become an active and interested participant in the solution of the complicated problems in our region: building a safe and stable peace, and protecting the environment.

Relations between the countries of the former Soviet Union occupy a special place in the solution of regional stability issues and in the development of integration processes at the regional level. The Commonwealth of Independent States (CIS) was set up in December 1991. The years since then have confirmed that there are vast opportunities for mutually beneficial co-operation within the CIS on the basis of equitable bilateral and multilateral partnership-agreements. In the foundation of such co-operation there are involved not only territorial proximity and economic contacts, but also deep historical roots, cultural and spiritual links, and the common fate of these nations over many centuries.

Rapprochement between these nations is a natural historical process. It has always existed irrespective of the existence of the Soviet Union. It is a popular and genuine integration, different from an artificially imposed political integration. It is noteworthy that none of the post-Soviet states is against integration. At the same time these states are not going to give up their independence. For us the issue is not to choose between independence and integration, but to harmonize these two lines. We would like to view the CIS as the integration of genuinely independent, sovereign states.

Such approaches have nothing to do with certain political ideas about the so-called 'deepening integration of the CIS countries'. Some time has now passed since the Treaty of the Four (Russia, Kazakhstan, Kyrgyzstan, Belarus) and the Treaty of the Two (Russia and Belarus) were signed. I would like to stress that the signing of these Treaties and their implementation is the internal affair of these states. Each state, looking at its own interests, decides its own destiny and prospects and is entitled to adopt and sign any documents and interstate agreements. And nobody has the right to interfere in this process, which is a matter of voluntary action.

In this case the question of whether these documents and treaties are acceptable to Uzbekistan arises. Can Uzbekistan join these treaties? We are constantly and pressingly invited, after all, to sign these documents relating to the creation of so-called Communities or Unions of Integrated States, while the question of whether or not it would be beneficial to Uzbekistan is decided by others, not by Uzbekistan itself.

That is why, taking into account our vision of integration and co-operation processes, any bloc-like interstate approaches and restrictions on free co-operation with all interested states of good will are unacceptable. Such Unions or Communities are also definitely unacceptable to Uzbekistan.

The basic strategic issue that worries independent Uzbekistan is how to prevent the reanimation of the old empire system. Unfortunately, we have serious grounds for such concerns because they are found in approved documents, in arguments and in statements.

What are they like?

1. There are statements that the CIS today does not meet the needs for which it was created, that this ambiguous association finds it difficult to make any decisions and that approved decisions are not implemented.

Certainly, there is reason for such statements. Instead of setting up feasible mechanisms to ensure the execution of decisions adopted by the CIS by promoting bilateral relations between the member states and giving them a definite form and content, there are manifestations of nostalgia for the old days. There is a desire to create supra-state structures: parliamentary, legislative, executive – Coordination or Supreme Council, Executive or Administrative Committee with a huge number of employees, unified military and political structures and so on. Deeply rooted rules and ordinances still affect our mentality, from the time when the Center could solve all problems and issues in the vast territory of the former Union.

For some reason it is believed that if an interstate association is created, it necessarily should have corresponding power and management bodies. It is no surprise that an analysis of the agenda of the latest meetings of the heads of state and government and other CIS structures reveals one tendency: to replace the urgent problems of economic and humanitarian integration with military and political issues, issues concerned with setting up a unified command, a joint border-protection force and so forth. It should be clear to all that, in setting up within the Commonwealth supra-state structures vested with the right to make direct-action decisions which are mandatory for all bodies and organizations, by-passing the relevant legitimate bodies of each individual Treaty member state, it would be very difficult to call these states sovereign and independent.

The linkage of every individual state, of its authorized and legitimate legislative, executive, military, political and judicial bodies with new supra-state structures may be metaphorically compared with communicating ships. The more powers any supra-structure of the alleged Commonwealth claims, the fewer powers and rights each sovereign state will retain. This is an undeniable truth. When we are assured that a Community with supra-state structures can be created where every individual member state completely retains its sovereignty and independence, we cannot take this seriously.

Take for example the agreements between Russia and Belarus. The leaders of both countries have declared that their final objective is a unified state or some form of confederation or federation. As a matter of fact we see that such unions meet the strategic goals of great-power communist and patriotic forces: backed up by the Union of Russia and Belarus to force Ukraine to join it, and after that from the position of the so-called Slavic Union to dictate their will to other sovereign states in post-Soviet territory, trying to bring back lost opportunities in world politics. For Uzbekistan, which is following its strategic course towards economic and political integration with the greater world, this approach is absolutely unacceptable.

And finally: nothing will prevent us from deepening economic and financial integration, and from solving in a civilized manner payments and other issues to remove obstacles on the road to economic and humanitarian integration according to the approved CIS Charter. Thus it is not necessary to sign agreements and join various Unions of a predominantly geopolitical character.

2. An attempt is being made to convince everyone that the main evil, the main source of the present crisis, of the disastrous living standards of the people, is the break-up of economic and co-operational links among the Republics. This is an obvious ploy to distract people's attention from the real causes of the crisis that plagues all post-Soviet territory.

It is now quite obvious that the main cause of economic crisis in post-Soviet states is the break-up of the obsolete ideology of the totalitarian, administrative-command and central-distribution system, and the difficult transition to new market relations, to a free economy, a difficulty that is common today all over the world.

This is the only explanation for why numerous enterprises in many countries of the former Soviet Union are in such a poor situation – have practically stopped operating. Many of them are paralyzed not because their links with enterprises in other sovereign states have been broken or inactivated. Hundreds of enterprises that absolutely never depended on co-operational links outside their respective countries have also come to a standstill.

The reasons are completely different. They cannot manage to adapt themselves to new conditions, to find markets for their products; they have no funds for their production and development. The problem is not that the links are broken. It is that it is necessary to reform the economy more rapidly, to upgrade payment mechanisms – to put things on a straightforward, civilised footing.

3. The following argument is frequently proposed by promoters of 'deep integration': they allege that integration is regarded all over the world as a characteristic process for many regions on the Earth. They mostly refer to the experience of the European Union.

Of course, the present-day historical development of all states shows that they are interrelated and depend on each other. It would be rather difficult to find on the world map a state that is absolutely isolated from others — particularly from neighboring states. In fact, integration and co-operation are basic principles of the European Union. But the European Union's approach to integration processes is based on the principles of the complete sovereignty of individual states, their free consent and respect for their rights. Nobody denies, of course, that the principles on which the European Union is built may be attractive for CIS countries, but there are five matters of fact that strikingly differentiate the European Union from the situation in post-Soviet territory:

First, and this is the most important, the formation of the European Union has a long history dating back five decades, and the Maastricht agreements are the result of significant efforts made by member states. No *political* decision can take the place of natural stages of economic integration, which take decades to reach an agreed form. Integration that is carried out in a shorter time must be treated either as a military-political union or as a political 'gobbling up'.

Second, the European Union has consolidated countries with stable, solid, democratic social and state structures, and strong, mature market and legal standards, mechanisms and infrastructure.

Third, democratic institutions and values are deeply rooted in the social consciousness of the majority of the population in these countries.

Fourth, the majority of the European Union's countries have approximately equal and high enough economic potential. There are no states that are patently advantaged in their development.

Fifth, given the relatively new foundations of independent Uzbekistan's technological and economic base, an attempt to join and become secluded in Unions within the limits of the former USSR is nothing but a policy for the sake of some obsolete ideological stereotypes – dooming ourselves to vegetate in the backyards of the world economy.

I would like to underline that alongside the European Union, and sharing with it management structures that are formed and electorally-approved by member states, there are also the experiences of countries in South-East Asia and the Asian Pacific region, whose ASEAN and APEC have no supra-national parliament, Councils of Ministers or other unified structures.

As far as integration on the level of Central Asian countries is concerned, it has its own specific features. This integration has always been and remains in its essence a shared matter for all the peoples of the region. Throughout its history the peoples of this region have struggled shoulder to shoulder against domination by foreign conquerors. Leaders of these peoples have always been guided by the ideas of independence and the creation of independent states. These peoples have been living in a vast territory called Turkestan for centuries.

It is necessary to note that the integration of the nations of Central Asia is not a dream or a project for the future: it is a reality which needs only organizational, legal and political forms. We regard Central Asian integration as an objective necessity, conditioned by a common territory, a common means of communication, the basic and leading branches of their economies, a need for joint exploitation of water and energy objects, and the provision of energy resources – to say nothing about our common culture, language and spiritual values, about our deep, penetrating, intertwining common roots.

This region has always been integrated in one way or another. The nations of Central Asia fully understood the need to rebuild their future with joint efforts after they gained their independence. The signing of the Agreement to create a unified economic zone among these sovereign Central Asian states by the Presidents of Kazakhstan, Kyrgyzstan and Uzbekistan in Tashkent was a practical step on this road.

There is a series of initial conditions and prerequisites for the integration of the Central Asian Republics. They require an equal starting level of economic development, similarity of social and economic problems, unified transport and energy supply communications and water resources. Then there are the general threats to the security of all the nations that inhabit this region. Among them are the drying up of the Aral Sea, drugs and arms smuggling, emerging terrorism and religious fundamentalism, and the threat of the escalation of tension and instability that comes from Afghanistan. Such threats, despite their apparent disparity, are unifying factors, because none of these threats can be surmounted by relying solely on one's own forces. These should be the guidelines to action for those politicians who are concerned about the prosperity of the Central Asian region.

There are grounds to look forward optimistically to the future of the Central Asian Commonwealth. The necessary legal and organizational base has been laid down: the Interstate Council, the Executive Committee on Commonwealth Programmes Implementation, the Central Asian Bank for Co-operation and Development have been set up. The program for the economic integration of the state-participants running to the year of 2000, comprising 53 definite projects, has been worked out to lay down the foundations of a unified economic area. We are very close now to the co-ordination of defence policies: the Charter of the Council of Defence Ministers of member-states of the Agreement has been approved.

The creation of the Commonwealth of Central Asian states in no way means their isolation from the other states. Neither do we counterpoise this to the integrational processes within the framework of the CIS. This co-operation is aimed at consolidating the efforts and actions of the states in the region during the complicated period of building up their state system and making their transition to a market economy.

For us the Central Asian Commonwealth is not a tribute to the 'integrational fashion' or a desire to dominate and expand a sphere of influence. It is our route to independence and progress in the twenty-first century. I am confident that the realization of such a community meets the interests of our peoples and will contribute to the strengthening of stability and peace in the region. The Central Asian states, with all their social, political, ethnic and cultural diversity, still when taken together form a favorable environment to resist the threats to their security from outside, and to support the sustainable development of the region. By this they help to strengthen peace and stability on a global scale.

It is my belief that it is not conflicts and hostilities that push history forward, but co-operation and confidence among nations. Security and stability in the modern world do not exclusively imply military and political factors. The economic, environmental and cultural components of our peaceful and prosperous common home, whether it be a region or the entire planet, are of no less importance.

Conclusion

When I finished this book and re-read it, while summing up its content again and again I asked myself one question: 'Was there any need to broach this subject, to discuss the complicated and acute problems that Uzbekistan is experiencing today along with other countries of the Central Asian region, in providing security and stable and steady development?' I concluded that there was a need for this book.

First, the very short but sometimes bitter experience of our years of independence needs an analysis of the road we have traveled, summing up our losses and our achievements. It is not an exaggeration to say that our country, our people, have never experienced such events, where each year of this period equals dozens of years, even centuries of our history.

Second, the subject we have treated – security, stability, the need to implement reforms, the need to achieve the stable development of the country and through this to provide welfare and a good life for our people, the need to take our place in the world community – makes clear our goal: to achieve state independence and sovereignty, and freedom and equality within the nation.

Third, a clear understanding of the problems and threats that stand in the way of this great goal consolidates and unites society, making it possible for every person to weigh and more fully comprehend his responsibility for and complicity in the (not always comfortable) history and life of his country, the land that is dear to him. Only an understanding of all this can give a person the strength and resoluteness to overcome all the difficulties and hardships that are being suffered during this transition stage on the road to renaissance and reform.

Fourth, I hope that all readers of this book will feel grateful to have now in their thoughts the history, potential, wealth and huge opportunities that our Motherland, our Uzbekistan, possesses.

Alongside this, I would like all citizens of Uzbekistan to have a feeling of sincere gratitude to their nation, and to all who through their labor and sacrifice have created the material and spiritual wealth and potential of their country. Our civic duty is to do everything possible to enable our children and future generations to inherit this country, this sacred land, in an even richer and stronger state, so that they will experience the same feelings of gratitude and thankfulness towards us as we experience towards our great ancestors.